HOW
COMPANIES
LIE

HOW COMPANIES LIE

WHY ENRON IS JUST THE TIP OF THE ICEBERG

A. LARRY ELLIOTT AND
RICHARD J. SCHROTH

A CROWN BUSINESS
BRIEFINGS BOOK

CROWN
BUSINESS
NEW YORK

Published by Crown Business, New York, New York.
Member of the Crown Publishing Group, a division of Random House, Inc.
www.randomhouse.com

Printed in the United States of America

Design by Meryl Sussman Levavi/Digitext

Library of Congress Cataloging-in-Publication Data
How companies lie : why Enron is just the tip of the iceberg / by
A. Larry Elliott and Richard J. Schroth.—1st ed.
Includes bibliographical references and index.
(hardcover)
1. Corporations—Corrupt practices.   2. Business ethics.
I. Schroth, Richard
Joseph.   II. Title.
HV6763 .E44   2002
364.16′8—dc21   2002003729

ISBN 0-609-61081-3
10 9 8 7 6 5 4 3 2 1
First Edition

This book is dedicated to the thousands of great American corporations that have created the strongest business cultures and most powerful economy in the world without going over the ethical and legal edges. These are the corporations, and people, that deserve investor support and trust. We will continue to depend on their leadership to ensure that corporate governance and managerial excellence in U.S. capital markets will set the highest standards and bring greater confidence to our system of investing in business. These great companies stand as a constant reminder to investors of the difference between trusted and proven businesses and those who cut corners and destroy shareholder value.

A few business leaders will view this book as an "anti-business" manifesto. We believe most will see it as an edgy but thoughtful perspective on the need to build more confidence in corporations and in their leadership teams. In this sense the book is a "pro-business" and "pro-investor" report under one cover. Corporations have some work to do to demonstrate their business candor and management capabilities because of what Enron and a few hundred others have done. In turn, we, as investors, have the right to expect the truth about corporate performance and the obligation to support the markets that have gained our trust. These times present the greatest opportunity our markets have ever encountered. If investors and the corporations they support can create real bonds of trust based on accurate facts and real performance, everyone will win. This is why we believe the future can still work for us if we will take the time to work for it. Those of us who are, at the core, dedicated capitalists will do what we can to keep our markets strong and to spread the wealth.

Contents

Preface

Competitiveness and aggressive business leadership have crossed the line, and our system of taking money from investors and reporting on corporate performance no longer works. The financial manipulations that have emerged over the years are no longer tolerable in the "new economy" or on the global economic planet. Indeed, the damage and upheaval caused by trading manipulations and accounting fraud, monitored by politicized enforcement, could be the seeds of serious calamity in the future. What is true about the troubles in our markets is doubly true around the world. The governance of public capital markets, wherever they are in the global economy, is the issue at hand. Reform of U.S. capital markets is almost an overwhelming task. The global extensions of this reform have not yet developed in the minds of those who have the power to lead the change.

We believe it is time to pay attention to these factors, and we have chosen to encourage a dialogue based on our point of view. The impact of the Enron case may cause more interest in business conduct than would have otherwise been possible. The big question is whether the Enron case, and the many others behind it, will lay the foundation for real reform. Unfortunately, the most probable outcome of this financial chaos will be the traditional activity of "study, wait, delay, and forget." Those in political and business circles most responsible for the "Enrons" of our time are the ones who do not want change. They will do their best to delay through an interval of time and other pressing issues so that reform will not come in any significant way. We hope our perspectives will add to the coming debate about reform and focus ongoing attention on this issue.

We thank Angela Tucker, Ann Marie Shattuck, Nicole Elliott, Adelaide Elliott, and Robin Moore-Schroth for their assistance with research, editing, and the calming effect they brought to our chaotic ways of getting things done. This was a family endeavor, so all of our children should be mentioned for their help: Justin Elliott, Tonya Elliott Lore, Elizabeth Schroth, and Andrew Schroth. John Mahaney, our editor, was a strong motivator, helper, and wonderful friend. We thank them all.

Washington, D.C.
April 10, 2002

Introduction

Capitalism rewards the companies who get closest to the edge, without going over, in order to produce earnings.

— Observation of a financial executive from a
Fortune 50 company

What must we do to destroy the integrity of our capital markets?

Nothing! The destruction is well under way. The underside of the stock market became more visible over the past five years during the frenzy of the technology and Internet bubbles. The markets, due to the lies of corporate leaders and those who surround them, are the casinos and dog tracks of this new century. The odds in Las Vegas and the odds of making money by investing in companies have two major differences. In Las Vegas, one can compute the odds of winning or losing. These days, the way publicly traded companies are behaving, you cannot. The dealers in Las Vegas usually do not insert or remove a couple of aces during the game, but on Wall Street and among many of the publicly traded companies, they do. At least in Las Vegas you get a good meal and free drink.

Fifty percent of American households support corporations by buying stock. But the level of trust people have placed in the corporate world by making these investments has not been reciprocated by reliable information about the financial performance and the actual financial condition of the corporation. Both individual and professional investors are becoming more cautious, with many reducing or withdrawing their investments.

We are beginning to understand the importance of verification, validation, and authentication of corporate claims about business performance. Everyone with an interest in our economic health and progress will demand sounder ways to find truth in time to make a difference. Smart, responsible corporations will help this process develop and become leaders in business authenticity.

Investors now see the conflicts of interest and the outright lies about corporate financial performance: the defensive posturing of corporations, auditors, politicians, and Wall Street. Their first line of defense is to placate investors by creating the illusion of reform—a lot of political talk followed by unenforceable rules. After all, much of the political business and financial establishment does not want reform. Disturbing the cozy relationship between Congress and the companies who contribute to political campaigns would upset a long tradition. Too much change would expose them and take them out of the game.

Managed mendacity, systematically applied to the investing public, has become the new science of publicly traded corporations. The one thing corporate leaders know for sure is how to handle the investors. They know just how much information to provide and what kinds of information to hide, and they can rev up the engines of hype and misinformation at the drop of a hat. Lies and deception at their basest level help the inner circle achieve personal goals of greed and cover up their incompetence as executives. Gamesmanship has replaced business management competence as executives and their boards have focused on managing the stock first, the business second, and strategic value last.

This pattern of conduct is not what investors came to the markets for and is the reason why many are now thinking twice about staying unless new methods of verifiable data on corporate performance are developed. The performance reports of Cendant, Waste Management, Sunbeam, Global Crossing, Tyco International, and Enron were certified as accurate by their auditors. But Cendant allegedly booked $500 million in fake revenue over three years. Waste Management defended itself in seventy class-action security fraud complaints and accounting scandals and became the most frequently sued company of 1998. Sunbeam was charged with accounting fraud for shifting $21.5 million from reserves to income to cover up massive discounts and inflated sales forecasts. Global Crossing was charged with Enronlike accounting fraud and inflated revenue reporting. Tyco International was investigated for hiding debt to make revenues look better. Enron and the others are just the tip of a deeply submerged iceberg. The root of some of these cases goes back for more than a decade. None of them received much attention until the Enron story began to develop and the markets declined for the second straight year. The sensitivities of investors have become sharply tuned, and Enron pushed the sensors to full tilt.

Enron and these other companies wanted to make revenue look stronger than it actually was during each reporting period. They shifted expense, debt, and sales forecast numbers from book to book to create the illusion of financial stability. They concocted their stories carefully, never stretching too much at a time. Their reports seemed reasonable, directionally right. Falsehood was concealed among accurate facts. The business leaders who were best at this deception were moneymakers on a "five-year" mission. Their goal was to manage an initial public offering, or take over a solid publicly traded company, push the stock to the sky, and cash out. In the process of making things look better than reality, insiders sold off at market high points to line their own pockets. If investors cannot validate the factual basis of revenue reporting, return on capital, and reports of cash flows, logically, they should not invest. But with all this deception and deliberate concealment, there is no way to validate all the reporting. This is the investors' "catch-22."

It gets worse. If only there were a simple checklist of indicators, like the following, that would give a signal that something is amiss:

- Abrupt turnover at CEO and key senior executive positions without convincing explanations about why people are leaving (Jeffrey Skilling, for example, resigned as CEO of Enron for "personal reasons.")
- Cash-out moves by senior management (i.e., insider stock trading in large and frequent volumes)

- Restatements of earnings
- SEC inquiries
- SEC warnings for aggressive accounting
- Reductions in shareholder equity
- Special and complex partnerships and financial instruments
- Elaborate compensation and stock options plans
- Missed earnings
- Complex SEC filings
- Sudden downgrades in credit/bond ratings
- Withdrawal by hedge funds

However, keeping up with the indicators of lies and deception is like trying to paint a moving train. Since the Enron accounting spill, corporations will move to other devices to play their games. They will be extremely careful in the future, and they will change their patterns. Any system as complicated as our system of investing cannot be simplified to a set of bullet points. Investors can't simply rely on a checklist but need to ask some hard, even rude, questions. Why hesitate being tough-minded when it comes to protecting your financial life?

RUDE INVESTORS

Individual investors have been left to trust the professionals—the fund managers, brokers, and advisers—to ensure that their money is with the best possible companies. Individuals, however, must still be responsible for their own investments. We need to let the fund managers and professional investors know that we now expect them to do their homework and recommend companies who are not hiding behind technical compliance but are willing and able to disclose fully what they are doing. Here is a list of questions that can be used to start developing an understanding of companies.

Basic Financial Verification

- How can you explain the last three years of the company's statements of cash flows and return on capital?
- What are the "off-balance-sheet" debt, revenue, and tax situations of the corporations from the past three years to the present date?
- Does the corporation finance any part of its revenue by providing loans to customers or any other outsiders?

Corporate Ethics

- What does the corporation do to ensure that employees understand their legal and ethical responsibilities?
- Does the company provide an independent "hot line" so that anyone in the company can report fraud or suspicious activity without being fired and with assurance of appropriate response?
- How has the company treated "whistle-blowers" in the past?

Management

- Has any executive of the corporation been sued as a result of business fraud or any other business-related activities?

- What do the most important customers say about the company and its management team?
- During the last three annual meetings, how has the leadership team responded to and treated shareholder questions and comments?

The Board of Directors

- Who is on the board, and what are the backgrounds, accomplishments, mistakes, and qualifications of the directors?
- How have the directors added value to the corporation over the last year, and what do they plan to do in the next year?
- Has the board evaluated itself? How?
- What is the board's point of view on the following?

  Executive compensation
  Business ethics
  Social responsibility
  Shareholder recommendations
  Employee programs

- How will the audit committee of the board ensure that audits produce an accurate picture of company performance? In addition, what steps has the board taken to ensure accuracy and exactness in all managerial reporting inside and outside of the corporation?
- How many board sessions are held each year, and what is their length?
- Does the board have outside consultants and advisory groups assisting them with their work?

- Since many directors have given the excuse that they did not always know what was going on in the business or otherwise demonstrated that they were not competent to understand the business, how do we know that the current directors understand the business?
- Do all of the directors own company stock?

This list is just for starters, an example of the kind of questions that shift the burden to corporations to "show us" they are right. If you can't get answers that satisfy you, then you know one, perhaps two, things are wrong. First, the investment "pro" you are dealing with doesn't have much in the way of useful information. What are you paying him for? Second, the company that can't or won't provide this information is suspect. As Enron unfolded, reporters noted that Warren Buffett commented that if he could not understand an annual report, perhaps the company did not intend for him to understand it.

Shareholders have lost billions in the stock manipulations because they had no early-warning indicators, or they thought they had the right ones but really didn't. Fraud is a game of stealth and maneuver. As soon as you think you know where companies are, they have moved somewhere else. To the extent that we believe what we hear from corporations, we are at a profound psychological disadvantage. Market psychology runs along a simple spectrum between greed and fear. The people running corporations have the greed; the investor just inherited the fear.

The fraud makers and innocent investors have a curious relationship. Like hamsters in a plastic ball, we all run with directionless motion unable to stop or determine how to change what we are doing. The net result is that investors do not know what to believe or when to believe it. They do believe, by now, that Enron was a culture of corruption. They are not sure about other companies, and they wonder what will happen next, uncertain about whether there is a reliable way to figure out what is happening in the capital markets or about having the facts they need to make investment decisions.

Companies performing well for their investors do not need to lie. The trouble is, sooner or later, almost every company passes through that valley of the shadow of poor performance and/or internal corruption, and that's when it resorts to lies and deception. This unfortunate behavior usually begins as a small act of stretching a fact or two about products or revenues. Stretching the facts eventually gets out of hand and turns into a big problem. Corporate lies are like the small streams and lakes of the Adirondacks of New York that grow to become the upper reaches of the Hudson River. The river grows in depth and force as it moves downstate, ultimately flowing down the west side of Manhattan, passing Wall Street, and emptying into the Atlantic Ocean. Corporate lies have small beginnings that turn into mighty torrents and ultimately overwhelm tens of thousands of investors. Corporate cultures condition people to think that it's all right to lie a little. One little lie, deemed to be innocent, grows—and then one day an Enron happens.

Little lies that grow into big ones are one of the causes of situations like Enron; planned conspiracy is another. Many corporations have come to believe that they can get away with almost anything, and weak enforcement deterrence whets the appetite of conspiracy. They know that the Securities and Exchange Commission (SEC), the FBI, and the Department of Justice (DOJ) don't have the resources to check on all the possible schemes companies can employ in the pursuit of deception. When the SEC does uncover a problem, it is too late in the day for investors. There is no reliable investor early warning system. All the bad news is after the fact, and the good news is questionable. There is clearly little deterrent effect in the way the enforcement community conducts its oversight of corporations.

The entire process of investing in corporate America is significantly broken, risky, and not relevant to the needs of a global economy. The progress of the global economy has outrun an archaic set of rules based on a politicized structure created nearly three-quarters of a century ago. Like campaign financing, everyone agrees that something must be done, but the entrenched groups cannot move. It is time for reform in the structure and processes of investing, the type of reform that can stay ahead of the maneuvers of corporations that lie to investors.

We are not just presenting some case details and interesting stories about corporate misbehavior, nor are we presenting a comprehensive case study of Enron. Rather, in addition to discussing specific cases, we explore the issues that must be addressed as publicly traded companies find themselves in a new context where protection on several fronts is required. Corporations clearly need to be protected from the damage they do to themselves when they provide false information, give less than full disclosure, and allow conflicts of interest.

Among the more than 14,000 publicly registered companies in the U.S. and the even larger number of privately held companies, there are a class of people who will lie to the public, the regulators, their employees, and anyone else in order to increase personal wealth and power. Investors want to know who the liars are and how to get rid of them. In the very near future, CEOs, boards, and key managers will find their records and backgrounds examined as never before. Both companies and recruiters involved in executive searches are now insisting on rigorously double-checking references, past employment and performance, and academic degrees.

Executives will have to do more than talk about their skills, experiences, and ethical beliefs; they will need to offer evidence. They will do well to think about what kind of leadership legacy they want to leave. If they are caught up in an "Enron," they can be sure they will not be admitted back on the field of play. Beyond fundamental issues like fake reporting and bad audits, a fundamental shift has occurred in the management foundation of public companies and the governance of capital markets. The forces driving the shift include:

- *Complexity.* In business, particularly in global business, complexity is becoming deeper and wider and is providing the hiding places for new forms of business deception.
- *Technology.* Advancements are providing speed for business maneuvers, both the good and the legal and the bad and illegal.
- *Inability to Grasp Reality.* Corporations are losing touch with the *performance reality* states of their business operations, finance and accounting, deal-making consequences, and the value of their intellectual capital.
- *The Need for Precision.* Managerial tasks require more rigor, more precision, and complete accountability in the boardroom and from the leadership teams.

Congress can wave its arms and pass a few more rules. However, unless corporations understand the new requirement for performance reality as a managerial task, congressional rule-making will be like firing a water pistol into a hurricane.

The cornerstone of the next economic period and the absolute minimum standard for corporate managers will be a new form of scientific management based on performance reality and accuracy in reporting on corporate capabilities. This is a management science and discipline that is possible, but largely forgotten in modern corporations. This is the management capability for advancing the best companies and checking the fraudulent. The growth of a corporate underclass is an important development in an economy that grows ever more complex. The capability for increasingly serious economic disasters means that companies that lie are the equivalent of economic terrorists in our midst.

Companies, even those that play games with accounting rules, still want to know the reality of their performance. They struggle to understand the details of counting revenue, cash flow, expenses, and a list of complex indicators that should tell them about real performance. The trouble with getting to performance reality lies in a jumble of different forms of measurement and analysis. What's lacking is a unified system of measuring and determining the reality of verifiable financial performance that is linked to actual operational performance. When a company can understand the combined effects of what it has sold, the real expenses it has encountered, and the potential consequences of the deal structures under which it has performed, it will be closer to reality.

Companies need to develop performance reality standards to bring financial and operational measurements under a guiding discipline, to provide more accurate, verifiable performance data. Performance reality reporting involves those people in the corporation who are closest to the material resources and assets of the corporation, not just financial experts and auditors. Performance reality defines an approach that traces how "performance factors and metrics" move from the marketplace, through the contractual screens and financial filters, and into the service and product delivery capabilities of the corporation.

The end game of the performance reality approach is the creation of information about corporate performance and the related reporting that is verifiable, authenticated, and accurate well beyond the standards we see today. This is the way to create a reliable picture of corporate performance and potential that investors must have.

The new realities of business are in conflict with a growing number of people seeking greater financial security. There is an aging population with serious amounts of money for investing, part of the record number of investors who came to the market during the Internet boom and the rise of online investing. While investors now want financial security over hot growth (they would actually like both), they are losing faith in the prospects of either. Their faith in future markets now depends on what action they see being taken to cure our vulnerabilities and establish a market that has high levels of truth in investing as well as good levels of growth.

Clearly, the Enron situation is a warning sign, an alarm, which compels us to uncover the bad habits our corporate leaders are comfortable with. For example,

CEO Ken Lay's letter to the shareholders in the 2001 Enron annual report contained a lengthy and heady sermon about the integrity and high standards of the Enron culture. Lay claimed that Enron was sponsoring a wide range of activities to ensure the social responsibility of the firm and otherwise protect shareholders and employees. Few, if any, of the claims were true. Enron not only failed to carry out these commitments, it was, in fact, incapable of this kind of work. Ken Lay talked about the principles of "respect, integrity, communications, and excellence." While Enron executives implemented none of these principles in their day-to-day work, most Enron employees probably took them seriously and practiced them. This is the ultimate power of deception, to cause good people to do the right things while those in power do the opposite. The executive team at Enron was satisfied with only the appearance of having said all the right words while doing all the wrong things—all to make investors feel good. In retrospect, in light of what we know today, anyone who closely examined this statement would not have been alerted to its incredible exaggeration. There was no factual basis to measure the difference between reality and pure fantasy. Enron substituted distortion for truth. Investors must demand that any form of declaration about corporate performance pass the highest test of public diligence.

As we look back at how fraudulent companies have presented themselves, we now see what went wrong: the arrogance of corporate management teams, and the hyperbole about performance and lack of facts. Smoke and mirrors stand in the way of investors trying to figure out what they should do. Investors are overwhelmed with unbelievable and continuous good news from corporations.

Investors hear loose talk and "trust me" attitudes from business leaders who drain value from companies and put investors at risk. It is wake-up time. Investors are about to learn how to break the mirrors and blow the smoke away.

What investors want to find are companies that tell the truth about performance and value. Concerned investors just can't sit and wait patiently for the SEC, Congress, and the corporations to do the right thing. This book will help investors to inform themselves about who is telling the truth, to be less easily persuaded about what companies say about financial performance, and to probe for reality.

CHAPTER ONE

The Mechanics of Mendacity

What's that smell in this room? Didn't you notice it, Brick? Didn't you notice a powerful and obnoxious odor of mendacity in this room?

— Big Daddy, in *Cat on a Hot Tin Roof*

THE VOICES OF MENDACITY

Enron's communication with investors was exceptionally effective. Ken Lay, the CEO, was a very popular member of the Houston business community and a trusted leader. He used that trust to condition his audiences in Houston, his employees, and the investment community. The CEO talked about the strength of Enron stock within weeks of the collapse of the company, encouraging employees to buy more. Most energy analysts recommended a strong "buy" on the stock. Everyone, from individual to professional investor, bought the Enron story and invested in an empty shell. Investors swarmed around the Enron information as it was carried across the globe by all means of media. The stories were false. Every aspect of the momentum required to keep investors in the Enron market worked extremely well. One analyst, some journalists, and a few hedge funds and debt-rating services picked up the signals that something was wrong, but the larger market missed them.

Companies like Enron fall when they get caught in the trap of their own misinformation. They come to believe their own myths and lies and make bad decisions. The tricks of the trade are a two-way street and ultimately became traps for Enron executives.

It is a challenge to keep up with complex tricks once they are deployed into the market, especially for the average investor. But if you're going to stay ahead of the game, you have to start thinking like the people who are manipulating the market. Here are thought patterns, from inside the mind of a tricky, but fictitious, CEO.

The Thoughts of Johnnie Bondo, CEO of Red Rocket International

1. The revenue and profit numbers are dull and incapable of getting a rise out of the market. When this happens, apply a few of the most confounding accounting rules to make the numbers look better. CFOs can always come up with at least ten different ways to present the numbers, and your investor-relations team can help the market believe the fabrication.

2. Stay in touch with the lobbyists to make sure that all of the accounting boards and rule-makers keep the rules confusing and provide plenty of account-

ing hiding room. This will cost a few bucks, but it will be worth it because of the added benefit of providing political access on a number of fronts. You can appear with the powerful on TV.

3. Stay on the back of congressional representatives to gain their support for business and job creation. Make them believe that jobs in their districts depend on businesses having plenty of freedom and no harassment from the SEC and the DOJ. If the agencies give you trouble, call your representative and have him threaten their budgets.

4. Make sure your accounting firm understands that the other side of their business, the consulting group, makes plenty of money from your company and that you consider all of them to be on your team. Make sure they know where their bread and butter come from today and tomorrow.

5. Set a merger-acquisition (M&A) deal in motion to get market attention and use the M&A accounting rules to further cloud your real financial situation.

6. Engage your PR firm to talk up the M&A deal as if it will be the deal of the century and to otherwise point out all the positive factors in your business model.

7. Tell your tax team to figure out how to avoid all corporate taxes; they have plenty of ways to make this happen. Not only can they help you avoid paying taxes, they can get refunds on taxes not paid.

8. Use special-purpose entities, as Enron did, to hide debt, documentation, and create fake revenue. By the time anyone can figure out this mess, you can be on to other things.

9. Create complex organizational structures, and off-shore ventures to add to the confusion.

10. Don't forget to drag your board into your schemes slowly over time. Once they get exposed, they will leave you alone.

11. Prepare for the coming conference call by getting your investor-relations team to spend plenty of time with the analysts to feed them all kinds of market study information that has been prepared by your market research contractor.

12. Make sure you have friendly analysts on the call. Those who make extra money due to their links with your investment banker will understand how to help. Don't let the other analysts ask questions.

13. Get on CNBC a few days before the call with some kind of an announcement to cause the analysts to push the stock.

14. Remind your investment bankers and their analysts that you are trying to move the company ahead and now is the right time for them to be supportive.

15. As the stock moves up, make sure you sell a bunch, but make sure the world knows that your sell plans were put in place long ago with your private wealth manager, who really runs your personal financial program.

16. Make sure the audit report uses all the rules and produces the most favorable GAAP (Generally Accepted Accounting Principles)-based report possible. The GAAP is the standard that practitioners use to produce financial statements.

17. As a hedge, produce a pro forma report, with all the usual words to show that it more properly

reflects the real direction of the company and its unique intellectual assets in the market. Make sure the financial TV reporters lead with your pro forma results. These are the numbers you want investors to remember when the news show is over.

18. During the conference call, tell the big story of how great things are going and project a large increase for the next two quarters.

19. Make sure that there is only the smallest paper trail on the loans you are providing to select clients so they can forward purchase your services.

20. Get contingency plans updated to reduce the workforce by 10 percent and trim expenses by 25 percent. You will need to do this within the next sixty days as the analysts figure out where you really are and the SEC forces you to restate earnings.

21. Make sure your board members are team players and use their prestige to add credibility to the stories you are telling the market. After all, the board minutes clearly show that they are well aware of what has been going on.

22. Get policy changes ready so you can avoid paying normal severance and related expenses when the reductions start.

23. Start shopping the company as a brilliant acquisition target.

24. Get ready to resign at the first hint of trouble so you will have a better chance of not getting painted with the disaster that will take about a year to catch up to the company and its investors. By then your holdings will be located offshore or in your spouse's name.

25. Figure out your bankruptcy strategy ahead of time; you may be able to stay on the board and bring the company back with other people's money.
26. If it blows up before you can leave, take the advice of Lannie Davis, former White House counsel for President Clinton: Tell the truth, tell it all, tell it yourself, and make sure to compare your case with thousands of others that are much worse. Get the word out in a way you can control it and then hope that it goes away quickly.
27. Blame the auditors for misleading the board and the investors.
28. Head to the beach for several months and let the storm blow over and wait for bigger news to cover up what has happened.

While Johnnie Bondo is a figment of our imagination, his tricks are real. If we took a broad sample of CEOs and asked them whether they had ever played any of these games, we would find that most have in order to make the numbers look better. On February 13, 2002, ABC News noted that Andrew Fastow, by then the former Enron CFO, had been named CFO of the Year by *CFO* magazine for his innovative ways of improving financial results. Magazines like *CFO* would do a real service if they could name the top ten CFO financial engineers who may get investors in trouble.

Fastow knew how to make things look great. He was a great financial engineer, and he is not alone. The SEC has been looking at many companies, including Xerox, Microsoft, Cisco, and United and American Airlines, for a variety of methods designed to make results look better.

One trick is the "cookie jar" method of revenue reporting. This is a way of holding revenue in a jar, so to speak, and spreading it across reporting periods to make things look better beyond the fiscal year in which the revenue is realized. This is also called general reserve, contingency reserves, or rainy day reserves.

Pro forma reports are also a simple way to make results really look swell. A pro forma report, as it is used by publicly traded companies, is a "hypothetical" balance sheet. It is constructed on the basis of assumptions and estimates that are not presented to investors. Corporations use these hypothetical reports to present the best possible appearance of corporate performance. The big trouble with these reports is the lack of standards and criteria for the governing assumptions. The assumptions may be reasonable, or they may be so far from reality as to constitute fantasy. Pro forma reports can mix outright lies and fabrications. The investor has no way of finding out what is behind a pro forma report.

Pro forma reporting may also cover sales forecasts, revenue forecasts, and estimates of cash flows. If company A uses one set of weighting factors to determine its forecast and its prime competitor uses another, investors will not know the difference. The assumptions behind a pro forma report are hidden, and they are meant to be hidden.

Pro forma should be an automatic red flag for investors. Restructuring charges, complex and frequent acquisitions, "merger reserves," "before charge" reporting, and other off-balance-sheet reporting are all signals that it is time for investors to ask more questions about what is going on. These conditions of accounting and reporting have become so complex that investors cannot understand them. All of these complex factors can affect stock prices, price-earning ratios, and other indexes investors depend on for tracking market value.

Investors have been given measures such as the price-earnings ratio as numbers they can trust. However useful these traditional measures have been in the past, their efficacy in determining actual performance has diminished as the tricks of the trade grow bolder. Without verification of numbers and assumptions, it is difficult to trust any number at all.

James Chanos, head of Kynikos Associates of New York, testified at the Enron congressional hearings. He described the following six interesting steps for spotting the early warning signs of companies in trouble:

1. The "gain on sale" method of accounting allows companies to book profits based on the estimated future profitability of a trade made today. It requires management to make a judgment about the weights, factors, and assumptions they will apply to determine the impact of the gain on sale numbers. If they are reasonable and realistic about their approach, they can come up with pretty good estimates. They can just as often be overly aggressive and unrealistic in their methodology and build a picture of profitability or revenue growth that is pure myth. They can trick the market into believing that they are on a hot performance trajectory when in fact they are about to crash. When corporations rely on these tricky factors, they do so because they need room to maneuver. But, as we have pointed out before, they can use perfectly legal means to create perfectly false reports about real performance. In these cases accounting rules

and methods are the enemy of reality, and they need to be tightened up.

2. Lower-than-average return on capital, if accurately reported in the first place, is normally a good signal of financial health. At Enron this number was 7 percent, quite low compared with industry averages for energy companies and Enron's cost of capital.

3. A large amount of insider trading is, as in the case of Enron, often a signal of bad things to come and the reason why the SEC wants insider-trading reports to be produced much more quickly.

4. Projections about market potential that run counter to broad market research signal that a company is creating a fake market to gain attention.

5. Trouble with customers, poor press relations, and bad press. Even when a company is reporting good results to Wall Street and analysts are recommending a strong "buy," reporters can sometimes pick up on customer complaints through service bureaus and discover that there is a mountain of customer complaints about the product. This can be an important early warning sign for investors. Bad press and customer complaints come quickly these days through the power of the Internet and the many "watchdog" consumer associations.

6. Human capital flight, especially the abrupt resignation of top executives, may be the biggest signal of all.

Some of these indicators are the result of games companies play to deal with the pressures of quarterly reporting to the street. Executives find themselves looking for every kind of explanation they can use to tell their story. If things are good, then how will they keep things improving? If things are bad, what's the story that good times are coming soon?

OTHER LITTLE SECRETS

In an October 21, 2001, *New York Times* article, "Time to Look at Stock Options Real Costs," Gretchen Morgenson provided insight about how options are accounted for as a hidden expense. Options have become the drug of choice used to keep existing talent and seduce the bright young stars of the future. When companies set out to recruit top talent, they assume that a large options package is the only way to land them and to get them to stay. Options packages became the scorecard for the executive team. Executives compare notes with their buddies in other companies and extract information from executive recruiters, and the result is an options frenzy. The costs have to be dealt with somewhere in the corporate books. As options deals moved down the food chain and were offered to more and more employees, the expenses grew. As companies went on spending sprees and then saw the market move down a little, there was a need to do something with these considerable expense spikes on the books.

In addition to creating expense lines on corporate books, options also became the most efficient way to transfer wealth from shareholders to executives. The options gold rush is not over. Today, newly recruited executives still expect and demand hundreds of thousands of discounted options just to walk through the door.

Management teams and directors do not want to see any changes in this game and have gone to their favorite political friends to seek protection.

According to the *Times* article, Representative Michael G. Oxley took a stand against rule changes to fully account for options presented by the International Standards Board. Representative Oxley wanted to protect companies that have made large numbers of options available to executives. In the expense lines of the books, a corporation can account for the stock options they give to top executives off the balance sheet. They do not want to count them as a regular expense, and they do not want the world to know how many options they have obligated or who has them. Options are real expenses that can affect the balance sheet, but they are not counted against revenue in any way. Options are also diluted over time, but the level of the dilution is not revealed to those who have them or to the investing public. Corporations very often overstate earnings by misrepresenting employee costs in the options area and in the costs of employee terminations.

Mr. Oxley opposed the efforts of the accounting board that wanted to change the rules. He appealed to Harvey Pitt, the new SEC leader, noting that changing the rules would harm American workers in a profound way.

Corporate lobbyists have been at work since the early 1990s to prevent stock options from being deducted from revenue as other costs are. Stock options are relegated to a footnote in corporate financial statements. The values of options awarded at the nation's 2,000 largest companies were worth $162 billion in 2000, up from $50 billion in 1997. Studies have shown that pushing these costs off the corporate financial statements has inflated corporate earnings and misled investors about profits, according to the *Times* article. Technology companies are the big users of options and the big hiders of this expense. The accounting firms of Arthur Andersen and Deloitte & Touche believe the costs of options should be charged to the income statement. The lobbying groups apparently want accounting rules to protect a few at the top. Gretchen Morgenson provides a great summary of the issue in her article: "So there is the mantra of the bull-market-at-any-cost crowd. Telling the truth will cost upheaval in the stock market. Stock prices must be held aloft, even if by lies. Never mind that lying is what really roils stocks. Lying about earnings, costs or rosy outlooks only creates inflated expectations. And as we've learned lately, anything that's inflated tends to deflate. Sooner or later."

AUTHORIZED FICTION AND THE PRO FORMA REPORT

If you need an acceptable report in which to hide such things as option expenses, the pro forma report is the way to do it. This "Alice in Wonderland" homemade report makes other off-balance-sheet mysteries seem highly logical. A pro forma report is nothing more than a homemade spreadsheet whereby one can make the balance sheet come out any way one wishes. It is a written or published "best guess or estimate" of how a company is performing or might perform in the future. The pro forma report became the favorite instrument of those corporations that needed a big break in their revenue pictures over the last two years.

This form of "make-it-up-as-you-go-along" reporting has been used with such cleverness that there are companies today who really have no idea about what is going on in their books or what their real value is. Like the expense keepers who lie about expenses in order to make the numbers come out right, the pro forma people have elevated simple lies to a new art form. They begin with the doctrine that they are unique and that no accounting rules on earth can really reveal the wonders of their value other than the pro forma methods they and they alone have perfected. They get the business journalists to put out their numbers to millions of television news watchers. The announcers usually say something like "XY Inc. reported record earnings this period and is forecasting two strong quarters ahead." In the next sentence, almost in a whisper, the reporter will mention, "On a pro forma basis the company really looks gangbusters. Now over to Bill who has some stock picks this week."

Pro forma accounting allows CEOs and their accountants to produce all kinds of fiction, which is just what Wall Street wants to see. The pro forma method allows companies to dodge the accounting rules. Cisco was a masterful user of pro forma reporting, making it possible for an operating loss to become a profit. In a February 2002 article in *Industry Week,* John McClenahen reported that Cisco Systems had reported a net income of $3.09 billion under pro forma reporting and concurrently reported a net loss of $1.01 billion on a GAAP basis. Cisco's pro forma profit specifically excluded a number of expenses that GAAP reporting requires. In addition to pro forma reporting, it also subtracts payroll taxes from employee stock options in its earnings per share numbers.

If an investor received both the pro forma and GAAP reports at the same time, it would give them pause. Pro forma reports normally come out sooner and move the markets before GAAP reality catches up.

IBM lifted its earnings by assuming it would pay less into its pension fund. Motorola boosted sales by lending huge sums to customers. Yahoo presented results that were 35 percent better than under GAAP rules by excluding a variety of costs such as payroll taxes on stock options. Network Associates, Inc., used its pro forma to present about half the loss that would be required under GAAP reporting. Computer Associates (CA), one of the most often reported pro forma cases of 2001, decided to come up with a new business model and a new pro forma. CA was able to report 42 cents of pro forma earnings per share versus a 59 cents loss under GAAP.

The basis of pro forma estimates is never explained to investors. There are no standards for pro forma reporting; it is the Wild West of accounting. Yet companies can legitimately use pro forma as long as they also, eventually, report under the GAAP rules. In the interval between the fast and optimistic pro forma reports, companies can make their performance look better than it is. Pro forma is, in almost every usage, an accounting trick.

A May 2001 *Business Week* article, "The Numbers Game," reported that there are many other games to watch out for. Vendor financing is one. It allows companies to finance the sales of their customers. Companies borrow money, then loan it to their customers, who turn around and buy equipment with these interest-free or low-interest loans. The selling company claims revenue credit for sales, which they have financed. This is often a deal among friends. It helps those who need to buy equipment to meet their contract needs. It helps equipment companies who need to report bigger sales and revenues.

For example, Xerox struggles under a burden of $11 billion to finance customer purchases of its equipment. In the last year there was at least $25.6 billion in vendor financing loans on the books of the nine global telecom giants: Alcatel, Cisco, Ericsson, Lucent, Motorola, Nokia, Nortel, Qualcomm, and Siemens. The total vendor financing of the five companies with a base in North America in this group equals 123 percent of their pretax earnings in 1999, according to a report in the July 2001 *McKinsey Quarterly*. No one knows how many more houses of cards exist in our economy. This is the kind of legal deception our investment system supports and encourages. Obviously, deception like this does not promote the financial health of investors.

The beauty of pro forma reporting is that where GAAP rules may prevent or limit the way companies can display the benefits of financial engineering, pro forma lets them present what they need to present by packaging all the creative ideas they can imagine. Companies extend the life of assets, estimate they will have fewer bad debts and better collectibles, and make any other guess they can to help the numbers come out just right. Pro forma reporting is a great way to present these estimates, but GAAP can also be used. Companies change assumptions about the actual present value of benefits, interest rates, and expected returns on assets. Companies can reduce or eliminate what they have to pay into their plans any given year.

The real masters of these accounting techniques are the Fortune 200 companies. They have the staffs, the research, and the intellectual capital to squeeze every potential benefit from accounting rules and still stay inside the technical compliance rules. The technically compliant, however, can also mislead investors. They can create images of performance that do not disclose the real activity and impacts of their business transactions.

During the quarter they will then try to retrofit the bad reporting back into a GAAP report by stretching every rule possible. Sometimes they get away with it. More often, as the SEC has begun to focus on this games-manship, they are forced to restate years of earnings. Aggressive accounting, as it is known, can produce either a disaster for investors or an interval of stock acceleration. It is the investors who do not have the benefit, like insid-ers, of knowing the basis for their stock movement. They are lost in the information gap.

Finally, pro forma reporting is a great way to present sales information, particularly if it is not true. Fake sales are a great way to add punch to the revenue report. In April 2001, the *Wall Street Journal* reported on a case where 70 percent of nearly $160 million in sales booked by the Korean unit of Lernout & Hauspie Speech Products NV (L&H) was fictitious. PriceWaterhouseCoopers conducted the investigation to discover this little problem. According to the investigation report, the Korean sales managers, seeking big bonuses, used clever schemes that even fooled the auditors. For example, they funneled bank loans through third parties to make it look like customers had paid for sales that had never taken place. L&H had a long period of fraud on a global scale, and the legal proceedings are still in process.

Phillipe Bodson, the new L&H CEO, noted that the L&H Korean fraud issue should become a case study for business schools. KPMG filed a lawsuit against L&H for providing false information to auditors and otherwise pre-vented the auditors from doing their work. They used bank loans and other pyramid schemes to make it look like new sales were coming in. L&H is not the first com-pany to think up this idea. Several companies have used alliance partners, or friends, to funnel money into the revenue side, then shifted the money back out with interest to the providers of the cash. Eventually, the scam hits the wall, as it did at L&H, but for a year or two the sales look strong and the stock moves up. A few insiders walk away with money while investors lose a lot of money. Fictitious sales, like fantasy forecasting, help the books look good. When the revenue game includes all of the possible gimmicks, it is easy to prop up the company books for quite a long time. Pro forma reports, like official corporate histories, are modern fictions. They are not nearly as interesting as the fiction paperbacks in the airport, but they are bold in the stories they tell.

FORENSIC ACCOUNTING

Most of what we have covered about expenses and revenue recognition gets rolled up into a big report called the report of audit. The audit reports are supposed to let us know that all the accounting is as solid as a rock. According to the SEC, which does not have time to check the thousands of companies that produce audit reports, the entire investment world depends on the professional auditors to make sure that companies are doing the right thing. There is only one thing wrong with this approach: It does not work. Auditors have paid record fines over the past few years for not getting it right. In a few cases, they helped cook the books.

We now have a special audit discipline called forensic accounting that treats accounting and audit reports as pieces of evidence. Forensic auditors now audit the auditors, looking for omissions and errors that have served to protect the raft of lies created in the past. The advent of forensic auditors is just a reminder to all of us that there is no objective information or formal reports on the real status of a corporation's performance that can be relied on for investor decisions. When accounting goes bad, the auditors like to police themselves with "peer review" as a way of making sure the books are right. Peer reviews usually take place after a problem has become apparent during investigation. Peer reviews are a form of forensic accounting, but they do not help the investor unless the investor is in position to use the facts in legal pursuit. Every bit of information you receive from a company must be verified in some way. There are no reports or forecasts, written or verbal, that you can depend on with any certainty. The forensic approach to corporate information should begin with the disclaimers in the IPO filing. If you read this document closely, you will find that the company is saying to investors, "You cannot rely on any fact we have presented in this document." The irony is that from the first filings a company makes, it provides a disclaimer that is loaded with fine print to let you know that you cannot depend on any of the claims or information to be accurate. As it turns out, this remains the case well beyond the IPO. This kind of disclaimer should go on every report a corporation files and every conference call. The IPO disclaimer is the most truthful piece of information you will ever receive from a company. But after the IPO, it's all downhill.

These are a few of the mechanics of mendacity—the details of how intricate the games and tricks have become. These are fascinating games. Corporate leaders never have a dull day trying to keep up with all the events around them and maintain their stories for the marketplace. While Enron leaders were playing their games and minding the complicated puzzle pieces of their game, they were setting up a disaster for investors. Billions were lost from teacher pension funds and employee retirement programs, not to mention from thousands of individual investors outside of Enron.

MISSING THE MARK

Is it possible that we will miss the mark entirely as we react to the Enron case? It looks like there's a good chance of really messing this up by learning the wrong lessons. Some of the problems of Enron, the Internet companies, and the large global corporations with big supply chains may have something to do with fundamental changes in business models, which are moving beyond the reach of current securities rules. They have new linkages in a global market not anticipated by audit rules or SEC investigative capabilities. The business arrangements U.S. companies construct with their offshore partners evade the oversight of the SEC. These financial and business transactions are becoming more complicated and harder to detect.

Another shift in our technology foundation is on the way. The power of computing and global network systems at the end of this decade will offer avenues of knowledge management and business linkages unlike anything we have seen in the past decade. How the next generation of technology will affect the abilities of global corporations to escape securities rules and the laws of commerce is a very large question mark today. We have yet to digest how the first generation of the Internet affects business. Imagine the near-term challenge of trying to understand another new generation of even more powerful and potentially chaotic technologies.

Technology power and the linking of large knowledge bases will further stretch the business models we think we understand. The speed and "smartness" of advanced computers and software will allow companies to extract meaning rapidly from exponential databases of financial and business transactions. This fast and competitive understanding of transactions, which today takes months, will push the speed and responsiveness of business. Those who can afford the new power of technology and attract the intellectual capital to make it work will hold dominant positions in the market.

Congress may be content to react to the Enron case and the current period of low investor confidence with a few new rules, but this kind of reaction will simply lay the groundwork for a much more significant set of problems. Business will probably continue to outrun the relevance of regulation and enforcement for a long time. In the meantime, we are swatting gnats in a tornado and achieving unimpressive results. Effective regulation is built on a foundation of clarity in its understanding of the core problems and issues. Effective regulation must have concurrent effectiveness in enforcement and penalty. No one has yet completed the picture to create effective regulation. The chain of connected processes in business and between businesses and the Wall Street complex remains poorly understood by those who can lead change.

The congressional hearings have revealed, for the first time in public, a wealth of information about corporate financial activities. The information strongly suggests that complex financial engineering practices are widespread, and while breaking the rules, though not always technically illegal, they open up a Pandora's box of schemes for hiding critical information. Since so many companies compete with each other on the basis of the clever use of accounting rules and financial magic, we believe that the deception is more prevalent than we have seen. Deeper forms of manipulations, once revealed, will affect market confidence even more. The wider the network of manipulations, the softer our economic foundations will appear. This is the stuff of financial crisis. Most of the issues are bigger and broader than the focus of Congress and other part-time reformers. These are areas that will be carefully avoided by those entrenched in business and politics, but they may be the real hot financial potholes of the future. Given the great ingenuity of our culture, good progress in all of these areas will not prevent the art of the artful dodgers from finding ways out of accounting for what they do. We like freedom in all that we do. However, in the context of missing the mark, we wonder again what all this means.

In a wonderful book, *The Tipping Point,* Malcolm Gladwell studied the epidemics of diseases to find out what tips them over, what it takes to turn a small trend into a major dramatic event. He found that small changes in a complex setting could push things into an "epidemic of change." The tipping point idea in business requires that people, an agent, and an environment act together as the fundamental factors. What people do and how they do it is important. People carry "agents," in this case business values, and they move about within a certain environment. According to the Gladwell theory, subtle changes in people, their values, or their environment can tip the organizational action over into a new way of operating. Without taking this comparison too far, we think we see tipping points all over the business landscapes. Subtle changes in business values and habits, in the context of complex global organizations, are tipping our business culture into uncharted and potentially dangerous directions. We think we see other places in our society where the tipping point is at work. This is where Congress and others are missing the point. They are not looking at the larger picture; they are content with a "task" orientation and a linear perspective to solve one of the most complex economic problems in our history.

THE FINAL MEASURE

Our unfortunate conclusion is that investors have no choice other than to assume that everything corporations report or otherwise articulate is not all the truth. Investors must find ways to verify what is going on inside the corporations that hold their money, or they must decide that they have reason to trust the leadership team and place their bets on the people in charge. Warren Buffett and a few other investors have developed some strong methods of verification. Many investors just depend on people like Buffett to place their bets. This is not a bad way to go. Unfortunately, there are few Buffetts out there, and the one we like best will not last forever. Investors still need to make sure they have the best Warren Buffett they can find. This will require some homework. The real Warren

Buffett, as described in Robert Hagstom's book *The Essential Buffett,* looks at the following measures when evaluating companies:

- Return on equity
- Debt levels
- Changes in operating margin
- Capital expenditure needs
- Growth in cash earnings

Assuming one can find the real facts about these measures, it is possible to get a handle on where a company is headed. If these measurements are moving in the right direction, and if you have a way to verify the facts, you can believe that the long-term outlook for the share price will reflect the growing value of the company. The challenge today is getting the real facts about these measurements. These are the facts that people most often distort when describing their financial conditions and their forecast for the future. You can bet that Warren Buffett and his staff know how to read accounting documents. They know all the games about revenue recognition and will pay close attention to how a company deals with these events over time.

In conjunction with these commonsense measurements, Buffett insists that the leadership be honest and competent. Measuring the leaders and managers is of equal importance in the eyes of successful investors and business owners such as Warren Buffett. However, measuring the human capital factors is perhaps the most neglected aspect of investor due diligence. If you cannot figure out whether or not the leadership team is behaving like true business owners, reporting data honestly and fully to the shareholders, and demonstrating personal courage and innovation, you cannot determine the real value of a company. *The Essential Buffett* describes the managerial tenets you should look for and that will be present in companies that do not lie. The quality of their leadership teams stands out. Their people are smart and admirable in the way they conduct themselves personally and as teams of business professionals. They do not hide behind GAAP standards; they are most likely to go beyond the standards. They tell the entire truth, admit mistakes completely when they happen, and have bulldog persistence about correcting mistakes. If you know how to look for and verify these behaviors, you will be dealing with solid, authentic business leaders and companies who produce great value.

The first area of due diligence is the management team and its approach to organizational integrity. Investors should pay attention to how companies behave in presenting their stories. You should look out for all the tricks we have talked about, but look first for the positive signs of intelligent and authentic life forms. Warren Buffett is not the only person on earth who knows how to do this. The professional investment managers, many of whom now manage accounts through the large brokerage houses, know how to find good companies. They know the signs and signals of the "over-the-edge" crowd, and they stay away from them. They know when to hold them and when to fold them. The good companies do not stay good all the time, and the bad ones sometimes turn into good ones. It largely depends on the integrity of the management team and the business culture they create and lead. Finding the few who are most likely to succeed and tell the truth along the way is the work of the intrepid investor who looks for strong business leaders who will manage the company and its people first, then the stock.

There is a very real probability that in the future we will invest in a three-tier market. The first tier will be made up of first-quality companies, not just the old blue chips. The first-quality tier players will be known for their strong boards and governance practices. They will have reputations for accuracy and candor in reporting their performance. They will probably have captured the best and brightest talent around because of their strong business culture and their authenticity. First-quality players will dominate the markets. The second tier could be called the emerging-quality companies. These are the next generation of innovative companies who are on the path toward first quality. Their track records for reliable business results will not be as strong as the first tier, but they will clearly make it. The bottom tier could be called the casino stocks. These are the companies who are still playing games. They will have the weakest of boards, the lightest talent, and ongoing problems with getting things right. This will make it easier for investors to decide. We just hope we develop the capabilities to tell who is in which tier. Among the capabilities investors need to determine the highest-potential companies is the ability to evaluate boards of directors. Investors should begin at the top where the obligation to represent shareholders is both a legal and moral responsibility. If directors in the boardroom fail to set the right tone and ensure appropriate oversight, business becomes a game of chance.

CHAPTER TWO

The Art of the Artful Dodgers

First, the basic linguistic unit of speech in politics, all politics,
not just the Washington kind, is a statement that is already
somewhere between one eighth and one fourth of the way to
being a lie.

— Meg Greenfeld, *Washington*

Many of us have assumed, as former *Washington Post* editor Meg Greenfield has so eloquently described in her
book *Washington,* that the entire fabric of our political
culture would become completely dysfunctional without
lies. We have a certain level of comfort with the persistence of lies in politics, advertising, business deals, and
personal relationships. We expect and tolerate a certain
level of misinformation, deception, and exaggeration in
our daily rituals. Yet we still get steamed when someone
lies directly to us.

LARGE COMPANIES WITH BIG LEGACIES

We are just waking up to the issues of lies about the capital markets. We're now, in terms of our knowledge about our understanding of capital markets and corporate financial stability, where we were two decades ago with health, environmental, and safety issues.

Some of the largest and most important businesses in our economy have had problems with the truth resulting from deep and abiding cultural issues inside companies. The same processes are in play whether the books are being cooked, tobacco executives are testifying that nicotine is not addictive, the airlines are telling you that flight is really on time and that security is being improved, or Ford is telling you that those Explorers are as safe as anything on the road.

The watershed was the cover-up by big tobacco of scientific studies demonstrating the deadly addictive powers of nicotine and the health threats of the long-term use of tobacco products and the specific targeting of young people for the purpose of getting them hooked on tobacco through their so-called nicotine delivery systems.

The scope and scale of how the large tobacco companies carried out their campaigns of deceit was unprecedented. They demonstrated that large corporations seeking to protect their profits and business growth are capable of doing whatever it takes to protect the business. Big tobacco paid record fines and finally acknowledged the risks they brought to the health of millions of people. The most memorable performance was the picture of tobacco executives standing before Congress, each declaring that they did not believe that nicotine was addictive.

The big chemical corporations have a track record approaching that of big tobacco. *A Civil Action* is a book that provides a well-documented example of what the chemical companies have done and how they defend themselves. They have the money to drag cases out for decades if needed—well beyond the capability of most individuals to pursue.

Like big tobacco, the big chemical makers nearly perfected the art of covering up important facts about what they had done to the environment and to the health of their workers. Both industries are promoting the message that they have learned their lessons and are now trusted corporate citizens who care about the environment and would not cover up important information. They spend a lot of money creating their image of safety and responsibility. Animals now graze next to the chemical plant in the commercials we see.

Most business travelers constantly see for themselves how the big airlines deal with the public. The summer of 2000 felt like the worst travel period of all time. There were so many flight delays, cancellations, and ticketing problems that the public was getting fed up with the entire industry and its Federal Aviation Administration (FAA) regulators. The airlines blamed the FAA; the FAA blamed its modernization problems and pointed the finger back at the airlines for poor customer service.

The airlines' top managers appear to have used a particularly "class-base" approach to spreading false information to prevent passengers from changing over to competing airlines. This industry has a heavily compensated managerial and executive class at the top and a much larger lower-paid working and clerical group at the low end of the pay scale. This includes ticket counter personnel, security checkers, and customer service people. Top management, the ones who knew the facts about delayed or canceled flights, set up the ticketing people to lie for them. They did not give them the facts so they would keep telling passengers that flights were on time, not canceled, or otherwise due in soon. This form of managerial exploitation is the moral Kantian equivalent of treating people like objects. It is the highest form of human insult. The insult is passed on through the ticketing agents to the customers, who must be seen by airline managers as the lowest form of objects in the game of making money. Revenue protection is an "at-any-cost" game in the airline industry.

The flight delays and cancellations grew so bad in the summer of 2000 that the media took notice and conducted investigations. By the early summer of 2001, there were several documentaries demonstrating that United Airlines lied to the traveling public. TV reporters dug out the evidence and reported the details. Airline ticket agent screens showed that flights were on time. Customers were told that they were on time. Down in the operations centers, the airlines had the real data on flight delays and cancellations, information that they would not share with customers. They would knowingly tell customers that a flight was on time when the airline's operations managers knew that it was hours late or would not fly at all. They kept customers waiting, even after finally posting delays, for as long as possible so that customers could not change over to other carriers. These were acts of revenue protection. Airlines felt they had the right to take this action to hold on to revenue. They were not about to hand over revenue to other carriers when they felt the FAA was the problem. We now know that the airlines were cutting every corner to save money and optimize those flights that generated the most profit for them. All customers received the same poor treatment when the airline had to choose between them and more money.

The airlines came close to falling apart after the events of September 11, 2001. They offered scary forecasts about going under and lined up for one of the largest government bailouts in history. Within four months of September 11 and the American Airline crash in New York, however, passengers were drifting back to flying. The numbers of flights and passengers were down, but people were flying again. They came back with an awareness that will not go away soon. They came back knowing they were paying, as taxpayers, for one of the largest airline bailouts in history, and they were also paying already inflated airfares. Thus, taxpayers get to pay at both ends: during the poor performance of the airlines and when the airlines start reaping the consequences of that poor performance.

The airlines have made little, if any, improvement on what they tell customers. We did a personal test and gathered the real facts about a flight we had scheduled in advance. We then asked a woman at the airline club about the flight information on the screen that indicated that our flight was on time. We told her that we knew the flight was delayed. She actually said, "Even though the flight may be delayed, the information on the screen is correct." This is the new customer service logic of the airlines. At the ticket counter, ticket agents said, "This is the best information we have."

While the airlines told the average passenger whatever they wanted to tell them, the premier flyers who spent hundreds of thousands of air miles each year as elite passengers could call the airlines' special 800 numbers and get a more accurate story about flight schedules and problems. This was the upper class of the market that top management did not want to lose. After the worst year in recent airline history, the major airlines automatically renewed the status of the big fliers even though many of them did not fly the required miles. Those in the front of the airplane were seduced to keep on flying. Those in the main cabin were locked in a terminal of lies to keep them from getting away. These are "friendly," "patriotic" skies?

After September 11, 2001, the airlines told the public and their own employees that they were taking dramatic steps to improve all aspects of security. One month after the WTC event, we interviewed airline employees from the largest carriers. One of them, in a fit of frustration, said that she was considering quitting her job. After more than twelve years of flying and achieving seniority, the flight attendant said that the airline had lied to its employees about the layoff plans and about security. One month after the WTC disaster, the security codes for the doors into flight operations had not been changed nor had the control badges, and most of the security procedures were exactly as they were before. The flight attendant said that she and many of her friends were afraid to fly and doubted that the airlines, in the wake of their new financial problems, would do anything to improve security. Yet the airlines had announced to the world that they were on the case. Now, all kinds of new legislation to fix the airlines are creeping forward through Congress. Do not hold your breath on this. Congress will not take all the steps required to clean up this industry. They will focus on the standout safety issues and those issues that have political mileage. What the airlines say to the public and how they deal with the public will be left to the airlines. With any luck, a few of the underdog airlines will move to the top and get into competition with the big airlines for telling the truth about prices, schedules, and services. We just hope they will tell us the truth when it comes to safety and security. But how can we be sure?

The large automakers are accused of cutting corners with public safety and welfare, then covering up the facts while conducting a protracted legal defense. In the most recent cases involving Bridgestone/Firestone and Ford, the charges have gone back and forth between two large companies who were at one time close partners. Each now accuses the other of knowingly endangering the safety of the public by creating unsafe products, hiding the facts, and denying any problem exists at all. In the interesting twist involving Ford and Firestone, we heard from each of them about the amount of research they had done and how carefully the research had been kept from public knowledge. These companies did to each other what the courts would have taken years to do. By attacking each other in public they both suffered an immediate loss of market that cost millions. They destroyed profits at a rapid rate during a time each feared how the other would use the facts they had. Neither was certain of how much the other really knew. These so-called partners were not telling the truth to each other, and neither of them told the full truth to the American public. The lawsuits documented hundreds of deaths in the case of the Ford-Firestone ordeal.

Most of the time when a large corporation gets in trouble, it can protect itself for long periods of time. It normally takes decades for citizens to reach settlements of any kind with large corporations, if they settle at all. Individuals do not have a strong likelihood of success when they take on an army of corporate lawyers. Big auto, big airlines, big chemical, and many other large corporations have figured out how to drag out the battles, keep the news cycle short, and get on with business: the business of not spending time on these potentially ugly situations.

BAD INVESTOR MEDICINE

The pharmaceutical industry has a long history of controversy in its business practices. The industry is on the leading edge of drug discovery and must conduct its drug trials on humans before their research investments pay off. This is a very competitive industry and one that has made many investors very rich. The pharmaceutical drug pipelines of the past decade have produced many big hits for the large players. In the past five years, with the emergence of the Human Genome Project, the promise of even more dramatic discoveries and market growth are realities for this industry well into the future. However, even with the Department of Justice emphasis on health care fraud detection, industry players still fall off the edge. Monitoring health care fraud is about more than cheating on Medicare. Fraud in this area has to do with clinical trials on humans and the introduction of new drugs to the markets. The competition to get new drugs into the market is the area where the problems most often arise. However, other areas of fraud have been targets for decades and continue to show up.

Abbot Laboratories and Takeda Chemical Industries of Japan agreed to pay over $800 million to settle criminal and civil charges that their joint venture had illegally manipulated the Medicare and Medicaid programs. Other drug companies are being looked at for similar practices, including Bristol-Myers Squibb and Schreing-Plough, which are being investigated by the same prosecutors. The Abbot/Takeda settlement is one of the largest for health care. The joint venture gave doctors free samples of drugs and then helped them get government reimbursements at hundreds of dollars for each dose. This was a kickback program designed to encourage doctors to push a particular drug. Six current and former employees were indicted on conspiracies involving kickbacks for doctors. This case took four years to bring to settlement and involved a U.S. and a Japanese company.

The company officials at Abbott noted only that they had engaged in "inappropriate market practices." These cases have almost no visibility until we read about the settlement in the news. Investors do not have a way to figure out when and if a company is engaging in "inappropriate" market practices that might result in a megafine. Who should know about these practices inside the company? The CEO, Executive Vice President of Sales, and members of the board of directors, one would expect. The questions about what the executives knew and when they knew it is similar to questions raised during the Enron investigations.

The large drug companies are now worried about revenue growth in the years ahead. Growth through mergers and acquisitions is slowing down, and consolidation has just about hit the wall as a way to produce growth. Since the average time to market for new drugs is more than ten years and costs around $700 million for each new drug, these companies feel the pressure to keep the growth record as it was and keep investors in the market. They have a big focus on marketing, sales, and revenue growth around the world. When these kinds of pressures are high, you should expect to see shortcuts take place. These illegal shortcuts signal changes in the culture due to pressures from the market. Sometimes companies collaborate in ways to make money. Collaboration can be an effective business model. It can also become a hiding place for fraud.

In May 1999, Hoffman-LaRoche LTD and BASF, manufacturers of vitamins and many other medical products, were fined millions by federal agencies for participating in a global conspiracy to fix prices (four other companies were included in the settlement). All participants set revenue budgets, and the spoils were divided up to the decimal point. All of the parties pleaded guilty and reportedly paid over $200 million in fines in the U.S. Additional fines were levied in Europe in late 2001. Officials of the European Union described the case as the actions of an international cartel taking illegal profits from customers around the world. When the market pressures build, some companies make alliances to support their need for growth in revenues. Collaboration in the art of setting prices and holding markets is not new, but it is taking on new forms. This kind of market control collaboration requires a robust flow of information between companies. They must share a lot of detail and spend the time to reach agreements on how to control market share. Each firm had to determine what their share of the markets should be, the details of competitor prices, and division of labor between the price fixers. This required deliberate and special forms of research, decision making, and agreements to stay the course. This is deception on a global scale and could be the big growth zone for corporate crime of the future.

TECH STOCKS

The so-called tech stocks were awash in cash from thousands of venture capitalists in the last five years of the 1990s. The combination of truckloads of venture money, the promise of innovative technologies, and outlandish promises created a sector that pushed the market to new highs. This phenomenon also locked down some of the worst habits of business management we have ever seen. This technology sector, the arena of high-tech precision, became the arena of slick marketing and half-baked ideas. Business plans, on average, were half true. Investors were left to figure out which half.

Few of the stock pundits and technology writers figured out how soft the foundations were. Cliff Stoll, author of *Silicon Snake Oil,* and a few others suggested that things could go wrong in the tech sector.

Tech stocks sucked up billions in venture capital and investor money, and their values were inflated for years. When they blew up, we saw how big the fake value bubbles really were. By 2001 hundreds of tech stock and Internet companies were failing and in bankruptcy. More than 537 Internet companies failed in 2001, twice as many as in the preceding year, and the numbers are still growing. In the rubble of these failures we are finding that they did not make as much money, produce as much value, or achieve the results they had reported. They had predicted, not reported, how things were, and many of us saw our money go out the door. Some played financial games along the way and have seen legal action about their bad business practices. Class-action suits pop up when the right group of investors has reason to believe that they got screwed while the management team pulled off a stock pump. "Pump and dump," as it is known on the street, is the manipulation of stock by insiders at the top to produce value for their personal pocketbooks. 3COM settled a class-action suit in November 2000 costing $259 million, arising out of its merger with USRobotics. There was no admission of liability on the part of the company. Shareholders filed four suits, charging securities fraud and insider trading in which the company misled investors to artificially inflate its stock value. Company insiders used $130 million to repurchase shares in a scheme to jack up the value of their own shares. Top leaders of the company then sold inflated shares to reap proceeds of $189 million. These are more complex maneuvers and require a great deal of time and attention by the management and financial teams. Management must be able to produce reports to analysts that will cause stock pickers to believe that the stock is a real buy. Indirect purchases of the stock and inflated revenue reports can be used to drive the stock up. When the market reacts and pushes prices up even higher, insiders bail out and head for the bank. Investors, with no detection capabilities for their under-the-table games, have just lined the pockets of insiders.

MicroStrategy is another new-economy company that practiced accounting magic. The stock fell from $300 to $100 per share in a few days following the disclosures of its revenue issues. MicroStrategy was founded in 1989 and created decision support business intelligence software. The products were solid, and MicroStrategy was one of the fastest-growing software companies during the '90s bull market. After new SEC guidelines on revenue reporting were issued in 1999, MicroStrategy continued to use its old accounting methods even though its auditors advised the firm to change its reporting. When the revenues were restated using the required guidelines, lawsuits claimed that financial statements were purposefully misstated so the owners could make profit from the stocks. This is otherwise known as aggressive accounting to boost revenue. This northern Virginia company was once the hot growth company of the region. The CEO, Michael Saylor, and management team attracted a lot of local attention and a lot of local investors. Ironically, MicroStrategy had developed software products to help corporations scan their financial data and understand precisely what was going on.

The SEC used this case in its annual report as an example of how quickly the commission detected the problem and settled the case. They did not mention the fact that many investors lost a lot of money. Once again, the quarterly filings signaled changes in the numbers that caught the attention of regulators and a few investors. The insiders knew exactly what was going on. Some people made money out of the trail of transactions, knowing that the stock would fall unless real revenues caught up to the books in time. The CEO and the directors took a calculated risk in the way they chose to recognize revenue. The risk calculation focused on the probability of the insiders moving the stock up and then cashing out. The calculation had nothing to do with the rest of the shareholders. Otherwise, management would have been proud to report what they were doing and why. In reality, management, not the larger body of shareholders, benefited.

Companies must face the reality of what it takes to measure true financial performance and achieve real economic stability. Stability is about both the facts and the feelings. We now feel that the facts are not right. And we are beginning to understand that our economy is not standing on as firm a foundation as we thought. We are going to learn that our economy has never performed at what we thought was its real peak. The energy devoted to playing accounting and reporting games continues to take attention and money from value creation. We have hidden value and hidden potential in most of our American companies that could be realized on a more level field of play based on accurate and simplified visibility about performance. We may learn that we do not know as much about real productivity and genuine value creation as our MBA mythmakers have told us. This is a mixed blessing of tragic discovery and actual opportunity to get it right for a change. Our first obligation for now is to understand the details of what has happened and prevent them from occurring again. We can no longer tolerate an investment culture that devalues our work for the sake of the greedy, the power seekers, and the incompetent. Mendacity must be rooted out.

CHAPTER THREE

Protecting Investors and Corporations

"They became like the Taliban. They were the holy ones. No one was as smart as they were. Anyone who criticized Enron— internally or externally — was taken out and flogged."

— Former Enron Senior Executive ("The Fall of Enron" by
Greg Hassell, *Houston Chronicle*, January 17, 2002)

And, no matter how many regulatory bodies the government sets up in the wake of the Enron scandal to crack down on corporate reporting and independent auditing, another company and its auditors will use creative accounting to massage their numbers. It's guaranteed. Finally, some Wall Street analysts will continue to act like cheerleaders for the companies they cover rather than detectives for investors. They'll gush about a company whose underlying fundamentals stink, but that has a close relationship with the analyst's employer. It's guaranteed.

— James B. Kelleher, *The Daily National Foundation
for Employee Benefit Plan Newsletter*

PROTECTION

Why do investors need protection? In a word, Enron—the
synonym for corporate fraud. We won't cover all the
details of this story, since much information is still coming out. While there are hundreds of other examples,
Enron is unique. It is the most dramatic warning investors
have ever had, and if any good comes of it, it may be that
it leads to the kind of reform that's been needed for years.
Enron demonstrated the power of the corporate lie through
off-balance-sheet accounting, fake revenue reporting, special financial instrument usage, and auditor manipulation.
The net result has been the transfer of billions of dollars
from investors and employees to the pockets of the top
insiders. Along the way the business leaders at Enron were
accused of committing acts of false representation, illegal
tax avoidance, management fraud, and fiduciary irresponsibility. Although it is a dramatic case of fraud, it is but one
instance on an even longer list of illegal, unethical, and
criminal activities that are going on in hundreds of companies around the world. The totality of the forms of fraud
and the impact it has on economies have yet to be meas-
ured or clearly understood.

Enron was the darling of the energy industry. For
more than a decade, it evolved through the ups and downs
of the industry to bring a new definition of what a major
energy corporation could look like. In its early days,
Enron attracted bright, young innovators who helped
develop the virtual trading model as a real breakthrough
in the industry. Enron was the new player and was very
different from the traditional energy companies.

The Enron story encapsulates the behaviors and actions typical of companies under pressure. As the company began slipping into difficulties, its problems were complicated by the actions of a few insider executives who looted it. These individuals knew that they had a severe debt problem that could affect the entire company. They fell into a chant of optimistic unreality, something not uncommon for executives under the pressures of a financial crisis that is known to them but not to those they have pledged to support. This is a pathway of psychological and emotional horror that rarely ends well. In a survival mode, which none of the top players at Enron ever expected to face, they began to take care of themselves and lost their perspective about the rest of the people of Enron. Leaders at the top converted the real value of business innovation into an empty shell of fraud.

Between October 2001 and December 2001, the once innovative and leading Enron Corporation had been reduced to a bankrupt and panicked organization facing criminal investigations and the revulsion of the entire business community. What Enron did tragically affected its employees and investors and deeply affected American business. Bankers like J.P. Morgan lost hundreds of millions. By January 2002 the top executives, including the board, had been strongly implicated in insider trading and knowledge of the fake revenue reporting. In that month, to further complicate the drama, a top Enron executive took his own life. Fraud produces not only financial but also personal tragedy. From a retrospective distance, Enron now appears as an insane asylum where the executive patients got worse with every passing day. Shareholders at the table of a fraudulent, crazy company are like poker players with a second-best hand. They never win.

Prior to the end of 2001, as the Andersen audit problems became more public, an Enron spokesperson reportedly noted that the company had complied with reporting requirements and that Andersen had reviewed the transactions. Karen Denne of Enron noted also, "To the extent that an investor does not understand [financial transactions], they are able to ask questions." She also said that investors who did not understand the transactions did not have to buy Enron stock. This was a statement just a little out of line with the normal Enron PR approach, but it was typical of the company's arrogance. Indeed, if investors cannot understand details that are false, they should not invest at all. If we follow "Enron logic," we are forced into the "catch-22" of investing. It goes like this. If you do not understand the details of investment transactions, you should not invest. If you do not have accurate data about transactions, you should not invest. If companies give you accurate information and you understand it, go ahead and invest. The problem is you cannot tell when or if you have accurate information. Is this really the game corporations want to play with investors? We hope not.

There is a lesson here, albeit one that cost investors and Enron employees dearly. Those who bought the stock saw their equity stake drop by more than $1 billion over the past year as the controversy expanded. By the end of 2001, and after several restatements of revenues that went back and forth between standard accounting rules and Enron's real performance, the company became a takeover target. The balance sheet restatements revealed that Enron had overstated revenues by hundreds of millions of dollars. The debt load, once uncovered, caused the company's credit ratings to crater and headed the company toward bankruptcy. As Enron fell apart, predators gathered to buy up the leftovers. The Enron trading system, considered the crown jewel of the corporation, was scooped up by UBS in a profit-sharing arrangement. Others took their place in line to take over Enron assets. Enron's stockholders had been pillaged by the behind-the-scenes deals, and the company's auditors had been brought into the circle of fire.

Even before Enron, Andersen had been fined by the SEC and paid large shareholder settlements resulting from other corporate audits. It paid several million dollars, the largest audit fines ever levied against an accounting firm by the SEC, in June 2000. Although Andersen neither admitted nor denied SEC fraud allegations, it also paid $75 million in 1998 to settle its portion of a shareholder lawsuit in the Waste Management case. Andersen also reportedly paid $110 million to settle a shareholder lawsuit over audits it conducted for Sunbeam Corporation. In the meantime, Deloitte & Touche was hired to audit the Andersen audit arm and its partnership activities. When auditors audit the auditors and still cannot figure out what is going on, you know there is a real problem. If auditors on the floors of the financial organizations in major corporations every day cannot determine the facts, who can? Between the distortions and confusing reports of the auditors and Enron officials, it was impossible for investors or anyone else to make sense of the situation. Enron had maneuvered underneath its partnerships, shifting debt, moving revenues, and reporting lies about performance for several years. The net result of lies built upon lies is that it only took some sixty days for Enron to fall apart. It was the fastest and largest business fraud explosion in business history.

If we take into account all of the reporting between October of 2001 and January 2002, the main themes of the allegations against Enron (as of January 2002) are as follows:

- Enron created special purpose entities and partnerships for the primary purpose of hiding debt and generating fake revenue.
- Enron may have been involved in the manipulation of energy markets in the western states and may have artificially inflated the price of energy.
- Enron and its auditors did not properly report the facts about company performance or the widening irregularities when they knew about them.
- Enron officials and auditors destroyed evidence of the partnership activities that were important to the SEC investigations.
- The Enron board and CEO knew about the schemes for hiding debt and creating fake revenue.
- The Enron board and CEO, with knowledge of the real facts, presented false accounts about Enron performance and its financial strength.
- The Enron CEO funneled money and business revenue to family holdings.
- The Enron board and several key executives told lies to pump up the Enron stock and sold their personal shares when the stock prices were at their high points.
- Enron has refused to turn over evidence to congressional committees.
- Enron produced inflated official filings and accounting reports presenting a false picture of Enron value for investors.

- Enron lied to investors and employees and hid the facts from federal agencies.

You can debate how much of this was technically legal. For investors, however, there is nothing right about this way of conducting the business of a company. These fraudulent events were made possible by a system of illusions. Enron was the magician, we were the audience, and we could not figure out how they made so much disappear so fast. Our concern now is how many more cases we will see over the next year. Tyco International, Global Crossings, Nortel, Computer Associates, and many more came under the close scrutiny of the SEC just after the January-February Enron hearings. During the first week of February 2002, as the market sagged downward, Enron was blamed for a loss of confidence in the market. Serious questions about the accounting practices of a dozen or more companies surfaced and further eroded market confidence. We know a lot more will be uncovered at Enron and at other corporations. The concern should be about the ability of the market to hold up under the pressures of several more Enrons at the same time.

INVESTORS AT RISK

At the top of the justice food chain, the Department of Justice's taxonomy of goals focuses on protecting the American public from crime. The first layer stresses the usual suspects: violent crime, the war on drugs, terrorism, and health care fraud. The next layer covers the areas of white-collar crime, business fraud, and government corruption. This is a logical ranking of issues in the minds of most people. However, the focus on violent crime, drugs, and now counterterrorism creates tremendous voids for the justice system that roll down into the budgeting of hundreds of government agencies at the federal, state, and local level. Violent crimes against citizens and the global terrorist threat are clearly items that concern the majority of Americans, but we should also be concerned about the other prices we will pay. Our war on drugs continues to be one of our largest investment areas and the most controversial area in the justice system. Health care fraud has actually been reduced significantly over the years, but fraud in this area continues to impact the welfare of society. Business crimes in all categories have been on the back burner for a long time. Until Enron they did not receive any persistent coverage by the business press or visible scrutiny by the government. Congress has not been pressured to apply resources in this area. In fact, the powerful lobby groups representing business do a good job of preventing Congress from taking swift action in the area of topside business crime and particularly in the area of securities and related fraud.

Due to the bad conduct of publicly traded companies, from the boardroom to the audit team, investors are increasingly dealing with unknown levels of risk to their money. The Enron case has jolted investors from their long sleep and made them question the very nature of putting money into the hands of a few top executives, the elite money professionals on Wall Street, and in the banks and brokerage houses. When those in the boardroom lie to the public about the performance of business and use the money professionals, auditors, and media to amplify their false claims, they create the "casino effect." That is, they reduce the work of investing to a roll of the dice; only in this case, the dice are loaded. When business leaders, their lobbyists, political supporters, auditors, and public relations teams knowingly support these deceptions, they are committing crime. They are putting investors at risk at a time when investors have few protections.

This idea of protecting the investor has never gained the status or level of legitimacy that corporations enjoy in our legal system. Corporations have been given long open fields in which to run and maneuver. They can legally avoid paying millions in taxes for many years. They live in a maze of laws that protect their interests and make it almost impossible to penetrate their defensive walls. They enjoy what even many politicians refer to as a form of "corporate welfare." We have created these extremes of freedom for business to promote economic growth. However, business leaders will say that government intervention and the imposition of layers of bureaucracy and reports continuously restrain their freedoms. Executives believe that they are suffering from disclosure overload, in terms of all the items publicly traded companies must report. Yet we, the investor, do not know nearly enough about what goes on inside the corporations. As investors, we have no way of receiving warning when a company is either incompetent, criminal in its conduct, or both. We find out, like Enron employees and investors did, when it is too late.

It is very difficult to determine the total scale of corporate misconduct around the country or across the globe. Since the SEC only investigates or inspects a small percentage of the registered companies, and auditors only sample parts of the books, we do not know the rest of the story. In the Enron case, it took years to discover what was going on and will take even more years before the full story comes out. In the statistics we collect it remains difficult to measure where we are in terms of the need for specific kinds of protection and the types of policies we should pursue.

Much of the SEC's attention is administrative, not investigative or related to enforcement. The agency writes letters and suggests corrective action. This "administrative" perspective has taken the teeth out of SEC enforcement and created a comfort zone between corporations and the agencies that are supposed to watch out for the public interest. In business fraud cases the public interest is best served when investors can receive a warning. The SEC, unlike the national weather service, cannot tell us when a storm is approaching. The CIA provides warnings about terrorist attacks. The SEC says nothing.

The dollar magnitude of cases has increased, particularly in the settlement of "megacases" such as the Cendant case, which reportedly settled for more than $3 billion; two Waste Management cases that reportedly settled for over $500 million; and the 3COM case that reportedly settled for more than $200 million. Most of the big money went to shareholders, and the cases were settled out of court and out of public sight. The megasettlements illustrate some possible themes of concern. First, the big dollars tell us that a lot of money was lost. What the shareholders recovered in out-of-court settlements was a fraction of what companies lost in fraud. Second, the SEC seems to be content if they are able to help shareholders recover a few dollars while the SEC also collects some fines. This is not deterrence. At best it annoys the corporation and frustrates the shareholders. Andersen auditors have paid settlement after settlement and, like the Energizer bunny, they keep on going and going. Dollar magnitude apparently will not slow any of the large audit firms and certainly has not slowed the rise of business fraud.

We have arrived in the decade of megasettlements and auditor fines as commonplace as traffic jams in big cities. Andersen and others don't seem to blink if the fine is only $20 million. But the numbers and potentially destructive nature of legal action and fines in the post-Enron period may take the auditors to the wall. We also may have arrived at the point in our business fraud history that offending businesses and their auditors can be quickly and permanently eliminated from the playing field. Andersen now stares into a potential future of audit oblivion put in place by still larger settlement costs and a market that no longer wants what was once a prestigious association. How quickly and dramatically things change when a company screws up at the wrong time. This little history lesson has not been lost on the audit firms left standing or the companies who have built corporate foundations on slippery slopes of accounting games.

The business intelligence gap ensures that investors will not have the kind of warning about business fraud they should have. It also ensures the lack of a sound policy basis to decide what the government should do and what businesses should be required to do in the future. Investors are beginning to recognize a distinct lack of specificity in the information they receive about accurate market details and about business fraud. We wonder, as investors, what other surprising things could happen to us. What if there are other things we should know about?

- What if the DOJ and SEC reports only cover less than 30 percent of the corporate misconduct incidents? This could mean that the majority of public

companies have many forms of "off-balance-sheet"
problems that make them appear stronger than they
are. They may all have more debt and less stable
business pipelines than they present to the public.
Who knows?

• What if it were possible for investors to develop the
  means to conduct their own due diligence before
  they put money into the markets? What if business
  intelligence were available from legal sources?
  This could be the basis for a new industry: objective, independent analysis and business intelligence for individual investors. Individual investors
  now have new, specific needs for information that
  is not provided by objective sources today.

These few points illustrate the potential shifts that
could develop in our business world if we open our minds
and verify the facts. Beyond the "what ifs," the worst
thing that could happen would be for things to stay as they
are. The very worst case would be if we create the appearance or illusion of reform without the substance, which is
a case we have seen before. The reason we believe a lot of
the "what ifs" will see the light of day is that we now see
signals about the future. For example, in the Senate
Commerce Committee Hearings of February 12, 2002,
Senator Kerry revealed that offshore tax havens and offshore subsidiaries were prolific. Exxon-Mobil has 140,
Wal-Mart 12, GM 316, Ford 73, GE 24, IBM 89, AT&T
36, and Verizon 21. Enron had 2,832. These business
extensions of U.S. corporations go beyond the reach of
the SEC. It is nearly impossible to find the details of complex business behaviors like this. Companies can form,
disband, move, and change these business setups at the

speed of light. Legal speed or enforcement speed cannot keep up with these capabilities. This is part of the new global nature of business and of fraud. Accountability has now moved offshore along with the facts.

Enron has helped people understand the nature of the problem. The concept of "protecting investors" now has a chance to catch on. But investors need to reeducate themselves about markets, risks, and the ways to find and understand factual information about markets. If financial planners and brokers want to keep investors in the market, they had better take the steps to create "reality-based" education for investors. Investors must get active with their financial planners and demand not just more facts, but a real knowledge base from which they can better understand what to do.

In the past, companies and brokers have arrogantly pointed out that there are risks in investments: If the level of risk is unacceptable, then do not invest. The problem is that no one reveals the real nature of investment risk, not even the brokers. The best protection investors can have is accurate and frequent information about company performance. This is what the law requires today, and this is what investors cannot trust anymore. Most of the information individual investors have access to they either pay for as a part of their brokerage account or search for in the business press. In the Enron case, there was only one analyst, John Olson, senior vice president and research director of a Houston-based securities firm, Sanders Morris Harris, who gave a bad rating to Enron. Consequently, he received a letter from the Enron CEO blasting him for his rating and reminding the analyst about how strong Enron was. Ken Lay wrote, "John Olson has been wrong about Enron for ten years and is still wrong, but he is consistent."

Ken Lay signed the letter and, in a Freudian slip of his pen, misspelled consistent. Bethany McLean, a reporter who writes for *Fortune,* sounded the early warning in March 2001, but the rush of other market news drowned out her warning. McLean wrote, "The Company remains largely impenetrable to outsiders. How exactly does Enron make its money? Details are hard to come by because Enron keeps many of the specifics confidential. . . . Analysts don't seem to have a clue." McLean got a hard response from Ken Lay, chairman at the time; Jeffrey Skilling, then CEO; and Andrew Fastow, then CFO. Fastow even flew to New York to tell McLean and her editors that Enron was in great shape. This important story had no follow on, and the public lost track of the big questions a reporter raised. McLean was onto something. Enron transactions in the public domain did not appear capable of supporting revenues and a corporate valuation that made the company seventh largest in America. The numbers were inflated and wrong. McLean was right.

Another reporter, Dan Scotto of the *Wall Street Journal,* was rumored to have been fired because he made a comparison between Enron and the emperor who paraded through town with no clothes. This story surfaced in Senate Commerce Committee hearings in February 2002. Senator Max Cleland, democrat from Georgia, talked about the number of people who had been hurt by reporting on Enron, and Scotto was included as an example.

Investors need the protection of accurate information, and that kind of information is not available from any source we have found. Until the SEC requires new reports, like the "off-balance-sheet" debt and revenue data, it will be hard to judge the real value of a company. There is no objective source of accurate and reliable information for investors until all of the corporate performance data and analyst conflicts of interest are fully and accurately disclosed. When is the last time you saw that kind of information?

SOURCES OF INVESTOR WARNING

Press coverage of business crimes has been virtually inactive compared with all the good news press. It is just as important for investors to know about every case of fraud as it is to know how the market fared on any given day. It takes a big exotic case to get the attention of reporters, and Enron is the Watergate for the business media. The facts about business malpractice need to be as available to the investing public as the dramatic news about new market opportunities. Warnings to investors should be as available as any other form of threat to the welfare and security of our citizens. It took years for the national intelligence community to devise the essential elements of information to support indications and warning. The investor community, with the leadership of the SEC, must do the same. There are laws on the books about providing warning, but there is no warning system. The government protects corporations from illegal foreign technology transfer fraud, but investors have no reliable protection. This should be one of our national priorities since economic stability is a major component of our national security.

On slow news weeks, we can get excited about corporate fraud. For example, the story of big tobacco has faded into history. Big tobacco, while paying substantial fines, is still hanging on and doing what it has always done. It is just doing more of it in overseas locations. We get interested if we see a well-known, or even a little-known, high roller get into trouble. The media kept the spotlight on executives at Sunbeam, Archer-Daniels-Midland, and a few other places when it looked like the top executives might go to jail. The drama of these selective events gets the coverage, but the hard facts about what lies beneath such events and how deep they may run do not. Since Congress, the SEC, and the press do not provide the in-depth studies on business fraud, our national understanding of how it impacts our society and lives is weak. The point is that the SEC must create a domain of understanding, beyond the academic level, to study, understand, and inform the public about business fraud. The SEC should become our best source of objective information for investors.

White-collar crimes are very rarely covered in depth. During 2001 there were a few poster boys for bad behavior, but thousands of others were not mentioned with any significance. There is a limit to what an organization like CNBC might want to cover. The focus is on covering the good news of buying stock rather than the bad news of highly suspicious corporate activities. Financial TV doesn't spend too much time on the underside of business since they make their money by promoting companies that sell stock. Business criminals do not pay for any advertising, at least not the kind that tells the truth. Business journalists have their place in the structure of our national business information network, but they cannot be relied on for objective news or coverage about business conflicts of interest and the full story about business fraud. They often get it right, but they more frequently get it wrong. They can be a part of the subject under coverage, or they can observe and report on it, but they cannot do both. Only when the SEC tells us the really bad news is it then reported. At best, these sources tell us when it is too late, if they tell us at all.

If the SEC were plugged into corporate transactions as the intelligence community is plugged into the rest of the world, we would have indicators. Technology has the power to provide real-time detection of potentially fraudulent transactions. Real-time reporting of insider trading, offshore formations, and revenue recognition can be organized into meaningful indicators and predictors of intent. The Central Intelligence Agency, National Security Agency, and Defense Intelligence Agency have been doing this for years in an indications and warning environment far more complex than all of the publicly traded companies put together. Corporations apply technology to solve these information problems for themselves. The SEC should do the same. Insurance companies and credit card companies use software based on "indexes of suspicion" to detect fraudulent claims and credit activity early. They avoid billions in losses with these systems. Investors, on the other hand, are kept in the dark. They are left to guess when things are going bad or simply to sell off stock after a business begins to decline. Executives inside companies rarely suffer from this kind of deficient business intelligence. Without reliable information, individual investors are left to trust others, such as brokers, or just step out of the market. As the nation gives up its ability to know what is going on inside publicly traded corporations, we will give up on the integrity of our economy. As long as the lies and deception go on, the "casino effect" will deepen around the capital markets, and investors will think twice before they play the game. The

SEC may have a new role to play as the objective source of information for investors and the stabilizer of our capital markets.

CAVEAT INVESTOR

The SEC was established in 1934 to enforce securities laws and protect investors. It came into existence because brokers, corporations, and Wall Street players had created an unfair and often illegal playing field. However, almost seventy years later, the markets are less honest, fair, and efficient in serving citizen investors. Investors and employees must beware of the corporation as in no other time in history. Investors not only get locked out of the real facts of corporate performance, they get deluged with corporate information about stocks and products in ways that confuse and misinform.

Business lies begin innocuously. Cranberry juice contains only a fraction of real cranberries; blueberry cereal has no real blueberries but contains other fruits and food coloring giving the appearance of blueberries. Like fake food products, business plans of new ventures are novels based on hope. Plans, used to influence investors, are based on the dreams of business planners more than market reality based on facts. Sales forecasts, deal renewals, and all the good things businesses say will happen to make them more valuable are speculations that are sold in the markets. Half of them are real and half guesses or myths. The message of executives about the strength of Enron stock was pure myth, but there is no warning about this kind of information. It is impossible to figure out what is fact and what is fiction. Our standards for communicating information about serious matters is treated the same as the trivial and useless hype about marginal products and downright scams. It all looks alike. In the business cultures of achievement and perpetual success and reward, people develop positive attitudes about everything. The corporate "can do" begins to translate into "I better make my hype come true so I will be seen as a player." There are few points for candor, bad news, and counterpoint thinking in many corporate buildings. Everything gets inflated a bit more each time it is said. Soon the thin ice of lies and deception takes over. This is a cultural and a leadership issue of the highest importance that has yet to be recognized appropriately.

The first decade of the new century brings together a unique set of conditions. Global economies are beginning to reflect the linkages that took the last 100 years to develop. Today, about 10 percent of the publicly registered companies in our capital markets are foreign companies. Their participation in our markets is increasing, along with the number of cross-border fraud cases. The financial linkages are strong and react to one another in good times and bad. International banking systems are host to international business fraud and money laundering and even serve as the conduit for a global terrorist network. The ultimate network, the Internet, has become the fastest-growing instrument of business fraud, lies, and deception in every conceivable category. Identity theft is one of the fastest-growing areas of concern for individuals. We wonder how long it will take for corporate identity theft to become a factor. The integrity of corporations could be affected by fake "cyber filings" to the SEC and other forms of intrabusiness espionage that discredits companies.

Internet fraud is not just the playground of individual scam artists; it is also one of the weapons of choice for big business, public relations firms, and news organizations. The Internet is appended to every significant corporation, including news/media corporations, telemarketing firms, and others who require the speed of computing to serve their business needs. Technology, with its new media capabilities, is at the center of much of the business information that corporations use to support their "selling" strategies, image making, and stories. The global Internet, in the service of global corporations and in an increasingly complex business environment, is our new place of business, where the old adage of caveat emptor prevails, for the Internet provides new forms of business risks. The Internet and other forms of computer and telecommunications networks are now, according to Department of Defense documents, the newest theaters of information warfare. DOD and other federal agencies are responsible for protecting our national computer and communications infrastructure. They have gone on record to say that they cannot protect the vast federal data files, nor those of the Treasury Department, nor large financial institutions. Information warfare is not just a specialty of the DOD; it is the way digital business warfare is also conducted. Financial institutions are well aware of the kinds of threats they face from foreign governments and business criminals, but information warfare is in its infancy. Large banks began writing down the costs of "hacker" attacks that transferred money out of banks over twenty years ago. Today, financial companies are under attack every hour. Cyber crimes against business are just beginning. They range from the creation of fake documents, orders, and data theft to the denial of information services on a global scale. The virus attacks we have all felt for the past decade are the first stage of technology in the service of fraud. The federal government actually does have a national warning system to alert us about hacker attacks and viruses. They do not pretend to warn us about other related problems. Insiders, in the form of unethical managers and disgruntled employees, are perhaps the least understood type of fraud in corporations. They have the power to affect the value and integrity inside corporations. But there is nothing close to the high potential for disturbing financial markets as digital business warfare. We do not know how it will develop and affect business and our economy. We do know that our levels of protection and warning are underdeveloped. Lies and deception, in digital form, are the unknown territory of the future.

CHAPTER FOUR

Words Without Foundation

The liar's intention is to make others believe what the liar knows to be untrue, and . . . the motive is to gain something by doing so.

—Evelin Sullivan, from *The Concise Book of Lying*

THE "LIE" WORD

Do we have any reasons to believe that corporations conduct their business with candor and honesty and provide accurate reporting to their shareholders? At one time we thought we did. What happened to the spirit of trust and the ideas of truth that we used to talk about so much? Those ideals must have been paper-thin to begin with because many now see truth as the exception rather than the rule. Enron alone has not led to this harsh conclusion, but the facts of life of our business culture.

We are a litigious culture. There is a bit of irony in the fact that, on an individual basis, when we are offended, we take legal action. At the corporate level companies seek protection from investors through rules that place investors in a permanent state of disadvantage. Investors who, individually, could never challenge a corporation and expect anything other than more legal bills than they could pay in a lifetime cause mighty corporations to cower behind congressional protection. Where are the rules of equality for the protection of investors?

Some companies played other games with the WTC event and the Enron case. Timing is everything, as corporate leaders have discovered. When the WTC event dominated the newspapers and TV reporting week after week, many companies realized that this was the perfect environment to downplay the bad news they would eventually have to report. This is the perfect excuse: "The WTC further depressed our markets, thus we must adjust our forecast and earnings downward. It's not us folks, it's just the terrible situation." This is the gist of what went on. Likewise, the Enron "news environment" provided cover for companies who could now develop plausible stories for bad reports or adjusted reports of earnings. This is not a form of situational ethics but a form of "situational gaming" where companies use the cover of events to maneuver. It is not illegal. It is just the way things work in the real world.

The 2002 reports about companies like Tyco, Computer Associates, and MicroStrategy cause us to believe that fundamental weaknesses remain in many companies with histories of good performance reports. Enron kept painting its public picture as the seventh-largest company, the "greatest" company in the world, with a great future weeks before it exploded. Corporate communications appear somber in tone, forecasts have become more conservative, and greater care is taken in the way companies present themselves to a very cautious investing public. In a convergence of cynical manipulation, halftruth, and exaggerated reaction, corporations are swinging back to the other end of the spectrum. Now, it will be fashionable for a period to downplay the company but hang on to subtle reminders that "we are poised to take advantage of the next new market."

Persistent crowing about how great things are by corporate leaders has been replaced by quiet discussions about hope for the future. Investor-relations teams and public relations firms are working overtime to develop themes for the interim period. Most of their themes are about "trust" and "reliability." They are trying to rebuild images around conservatism and "straight shooting." For now, these are "images," not reality. When the boom comes back, as one CNN reporter noted, "You can bet that they will all be back on the bandwagon again."

Bandwagons, like the new economy Internet of the past, will come back in new forms with new attractions. Investors, if not careful, will be back on the ride again, because often we move through periods of adjustment without really ever making the fundamental changes to keep us from repeating history. That is why we have more than a hundred years of cycles of business fraud in our past and surprises in our future. But now, no matter how much we are told that we can really find the truth by reading 10K and 10Q details and depend on the coming audit reforms, we must not fall for it. We must do our best to find out more about companies who have never had audit or performance reporting problems and have long and strong histories of results. This must be the new mode of operating when we have clear and present proof that companies do tell lies and do misrepresent the facts. We hope the new attitude will emerge to force the new age of scientific management and fact-based decisions. Companies need to be on notice that if they do not produce the real facts, they will be out of business.

Would it not be interesting if investors had the means to verify every fact, report, or announcement made by public companies and investment banking, brokerage houses, analysts, and business reporters? What if they demanded the development of a process by which truth and facts could be found? Better yet, what if investors demanded this as the standard before any money crosses the table? We think investors are about to make this demand. The brokers, analysts, companies, and financial planners who provide information to investors must get their facts straight. Investors are going to ask the old Watergate question in a different format, "What do you know and how do you know it?" "Has it been verified or did you just make this up for me?" Investors will listen closely to the answers they receive.

The SEC relies on auditors who have proven that they cannot find the truth. We all rely on business executives to have the ethical standards and moral courage to tell us the facts. How big of a gamble is this? It's too big for investors. Companies smart enough to lead the way in the verification movement will get the support of the new generation of "show me" investors.

CFO magazine reported in 1998 that in an informal

survey of corporate financial executives, 78 percent said they had been asked to use accounting rules to cast reporting in a better light and 38 percent had complied.

There have been several surveys about CEOs and CFOs cheating on corporate performance. The surveys were designed differently but all confirm the fact that there is a significant amount of pressure on CFOs from senior executives, and many of them fall under the weight of that pressure to present false reports. For example, a June 2000 KPMG audit committee report for the Audit Institute reported that 55 percent of CFOs fought off suggestions from senior executives to misrepresent corporate financial results.

In every situation where we approached corporate executives about the possibility of corporate lies, without exception we were met with such reactions as "Oh, could I tell you a few stories" or "We all know we all lie about a lot of important things, don't we?" They all told us, in fact, they could tell many stories about how their companies lied to the public, to employees, and to regulatory officials.

Their stories included facts about how they had created schemes to finance customers to forward purchase services and thereby jack up revenues. They told how they hid expenses across the books just under the noses of their auditors. One executive even seemed proud of the fact that his CFO had called him to let him know in advance that he should dump stock in a few days if he wanted to make some real money. Everyone can come up with a story: There are thousands of stories in the big city about corporate lies. Almost everyone can tell a story about how their company lied about something, sometime, somewhere. It is interesting to note that the people we interviewed figured out in retrospect that they were the ones most likely to be lied to first. Companies have a need to make the employees believe that all is well in the company and all is well with their job stability. This is the first set of stories, and it is first told to the people of the company. Once the company is insulated by its own deception, the stories move out into the marketplace and are inadvertently supported by employees who have become true believers.

These patterns of deception and business culture have deep influences over corporate behavior. This has become normal, accepted behavior in many circles. However, moral leadership maintains the viewpoint that behavior can be changed. It is our individual capability to not follow the herd and to remember the difference between reality and baloney. It's up to us to decide how we will behave in business. Therefore, the observable behaviors in the marketplace are the products of personal choice. This is another little piece of reality. Given the number of times Enron executives tried to excuse themselves from their responsibilities, one would think that corporate leadership is the land of no accountability.

It was a lawyer for J.P. Morgan who applied the concept of declaration without foundation as the legal issue with the Enron board. J.P. Morgan is estimated to have lost at least $400 million in a combination of investments and bad credit in Enron. A declaration without foundation is the legal concept or basis for the "lie." One of the complaints was that the Enron CEO and members of the board made declarations about the performance of the company without foundation. In simple terms, they lied about facts, figures, and situations that had no factual basis, and to make the legal point, they knew the real facts. The exec-utives then used the results of their declarations to manip-ulate the market for personal gain.

Factual foundations are required when you are going to declare or talk about how things are going at your pub-licly traded company. The bank's legal case is about its need to recover lost billions. The bank, like individual investors, did not do its homework on Enron. It was a vic-tim of declarations without foundation.

Enron employees who lost their life savings were per-haps the saddest victims of all. They lost billions in Enron stock because of lockup rules and bad information. These are real victims with no place to turn for satisfaction. Before more of us become victims, we need to understand how corporations tell us lies. We need a better under-standing of the information foundations that companies use when they communicate with us.

WHAT DO THEY LIE ABOUT?

Determining what information companies will share with the public can be either an act of candor and courage or an act of deception. The executive team makes hard deci-sions every time they report to the public because they know they have excluded some details and made their own set of assumptions about the facts they report. They have struggled to apply the accounting rules to meet their needs and to deal with the expediencies of the day. As the executive team settles into the quarterly conference call, they think they have covered all the bases and will be able to give the stock a "pop." This takes good news, and the news is not always so good. The reporting pressure cooker punishes weak stories and rewards the grand news of big projections. It takes moral courage to tell it like it is. Anyone can do otherwise.

The annual report is a prime example of a document of declaration. It is a marketing document, and CEO letters and interviews that are part of the annual report provide sound bites that cannot be verified. The abuse of the annual report through exaggeration and marketing hype has almost rendered this expensive document a useless artifact. Revenue reports can be based on any assumptions and estimates the CEO will allow, even in the annual report. Auditors certify financial data in annual reports every year that turn out to be false. Many times corporations simply fail to mention what is most important. The executives and their auditors make judgments about what is "material" and what is not. Often they are dead wrong.

Corporate communications are presented with authority and confidence. They are persuasive by design. The motivational speeches of Ken Lay at Enron were powerful, moving sermons designed to convince employees to believe in Enron and buy more stock. They did because he gave them a fake image to believe in. He described an Enron that did not exist. The biggest myth in his speeches was that Enron was stronger than ever. This was a message that he repeated during the period when things were falling apart. Enron was not strong; it was a house of cards. Corporate communications by a CEO have a double edge. The first edge, in Lay's case, was that his message was not true. The second edge was that longtime employees wanted to believe this good news, and they did. Ken Lay, in an e-mail to employees, was reported to have written, "Our performance has never been stronger; our business model has never been more robust; our growth has never been more certain. . . . We have the finest organization in American business today." Congressman Henry Waxman, ranking minority member of the House, in documents from his committee hearings, requested that Ken Lay verify whether he sent the e-mail.* Waxman cited many e-mails that Lay sent to employees about the strength of Enron. While he was sending these messages, he was selling stock and trying to negotiate his multimillion-dollar severance package. While he talked about the strength of Enron, Lay was calling Treasury Secretary O'Neill, allegedly for help with Enron's financial problems.

Any corporate leader can have this impact to a certain degree. The youthful Michael Saylor, CEO of MicroStrategy, has been written about as an example of how creating a "rah, rah" culture in a new company can lead to a big mistake. MicroStrategy under Saylor's leadership created a new, aggressive culture. He spoke to his people often and with great enthusiasm. His people believed in him and the mission of the company. They were totally committed. The same messages were given at regional technology conferences to persuade investors to support the company. Then came the mistake, an inflated revenue report that put investors and employees at risk. These motivational CEOs are the new evangelists for the gospel of false optimism. MicroStrategy was a start-up with big potential, and its management team created the image of a hot, innovative company storming the technology markets. The stock looked impressive until investors found out that the revenue reporting was wrong. The CEO and the board bet on a way of making revenues look huge and

---

*Letter from Henry Waxman to Ken Lay (January 12, 2002).

always growing and then were forced by the SEC to restate.

Important audiences are listening to corporate earnings reports about revenue growth and profits. The first is the universe of investors. The second is Wall Street—the analysts, investment bankers, brokers, and financial media. All of these parties, including professional analysts, claim that they cannot do their jobs without accurate reporting from corporations and auditors. Yet the hottest zone of bogus corporate information is in the area of accounting fraud. This is the high-growth zone of deception and the most worrisome area of business fraud. The number of restatements of revenue has more than doubled over the past few years. In some cases the companies were lying about revenues; in other cases they were trapped in the jungle of reporting interpretations and made the wrong choice. In all cases they transmit their messages about great revenue growth and earnings to audiences who are about to make million-dollar decisions on the basis of these reports.

Revenue reporting is the best-protected area of manipulation for companies who need to cheat. The rules are so loose that, in a crunch, it is worth taking the risk and getting a hand slap from the SEC. The risk, as Micro-Strategy discovered, is that once you get caught and are forced to restate revenue, the stock and integrity of the company may not recover. The CEO and the board still made their money, though. The art of capitalism at work is getting to the edge without going over. But the edge has changed, and capitalists *are* going over. The edge is the place where companies can go too far. It is the occasion when SEC-directed restatements result in destroying shareholder value. The edge is where a CEO takes just one more little risk in revenue reporting that takes the company over the edge and into the abyss of fraud or worse.

Executive deception rolls down to impact accounting and audit teams. The accountants get blamed for not telling or finding the truth. In many cases they do not look very hard, and sometimes the accounting and audit teams are a part of the fraud. At Enron, Andersen auditors were part of the family. Their consulting unit made millions by advising Enron executives on everything from tax avoidance to strategy. Former Andersen auditors were Enron managers who worked with the audit teams. This pleasant and cozy set of professional relationships and potential conflicts of interest created an "unprofessional" environment for serious work. Andersen has paid record fines and out-of-court settlements because of exactly the same kind of loose and lax auditing found at Enron. However, as in the past, when the news of poor audit work was reported, they said it was not their fault. They never said, "We screwed up." In past cases of audit-related fraud all accused parties took up protracted legal battles to let the clock tick on and memories fade. The time between when the executive cooks the books, exploits the results, and truth is discovered always favors the fraud makers. There is no real-time audit or any process fast enough to protect the investors. When or if the liars get caught, they have a very good chance of getting away. Time passes, and people forget the track records of corporations and business leaders. History is invited to repeat, and it does.

This critical business process of revenue recognition, reporting, restatement, and correction has a complicated foundation of rules and time. This is the area that is easiest to exploit by corporations and easiest to defend by auditors. It also happens to be an area where honest mistakes can be made. The regulations provide wide latitude and broad interpretation. Audit rules are the equivalent of medieval scholastic theological texts. The rules support never-ending arguments and ponderous interpretations. Like the thirteenth-century theologians, the high priests never get hurt, only those who are asked to believe. They can be used to explain anything in any way. This is the business process of greatest vulnerability and the least likely area of change, but if we cannot fix it, we cannot expect to improve the other business processes in which lies can be manufactured at will.

The first principles of reform in this area are simple, at least on the surface. First, auditors must be 100 percent independent. In the best case, the SEC would appoint auditors from a pool to determine the scope of the audit and do the work. Restatements of revenue would have to directly affect the compensation of executives in a more dramatic way than it does today. Restating revenue has become accepted as something you need to do now and then. Taking a "onetime" charge is something companies do over and over again. If a company finds that taking a hit on earnings for a onetime restructuring charge for acquisition costs or layoffs works well with the market, they will use it again. Behind the charges are others that may not be related to acquisition costs or layoffs. In some cases the real costs of employee layoffs are hidden in the books because of the impact they could have on quarterly earnings. The consequences for this kind of gamesmanship are not personal enough. You can bet that auditors and corporate executives alike want few reforms around this business process. These are the easy hiding places for playing games with the market. If auditors or SEC investigators seem to be getting close to figuring out what a company is doing with expenses, companies can shift over to another game. They begin to manipulate debt, or capitalization rules, or option expenses. Some moves are perfectly legal; others are perfectly deceptive and illegal.

The Andersen auditors have taken a lot of heat about Enron. The auditing profession has made its own bed over the past few years, and now it's sleeping in it. With Enron, though, the central fact is that the board of directors and the CEO were the prime movers. Corporate executives must be held accountable, since they are responsible for the behavior of their firms. Before Congress or the SEC begins to make more policies and rules about fraud prevention in large corporations, business executives and boards would do well to begin their own programs of reform. The buck stops in the boardroom, and that is where the cleanup must start. If the topside leaders want to recover from the impact of the period of business scandals we have seen, they will need to learn to tell the truth rather than promote messages of falsehood. They will need to find credibility based on new ways of communicating with shareholders and the public at large. Once they have accepted their responsibilities, they must then work with Congress and the securities agencies to ensure that the right rules are in place. Their collective objective is creating both regulations and accountability that will give investors reasons to believe that things will get better.

STAYING ON MESSAGE TO DEFLECT THE TRUTH

When you lie, or when you tell the truth, it is important to stay on message. Telling the truth makes it easier to stay on message. The art of being on message reaches its high point on the Sunday morning news shows when politicians pitch their fully spun messages. The way they dodge every question by returning the fire with the message they want to get out is a wonder to behold. Their message ignores the questions, the issues, and the concerns of the public. They just want to drill the message into your head, and the method works very well.

The corporate message makers want investors to believe in a one-way message. They do not want any serious form of dialogue, particularly questions about validity and accuracy. To not only change the minds of investors, but to fill minds with messages that are not true, amounts to corporate propaganda. If we could ask the corporate communicators one question and be sure of an accurate answer, we would ask, "How do you know and how will you prove it to us?" If people ask too many questions, they might get the message makers to tell more than they want to. They might commit the truth.

Both politicians and business leaders are targeting audiences, making a lot of public noise about an issue for consumption by certain constituents. The critical process of communicating with valued constituencies is a game of manipulation. The "target audience" is targeted to produce a specific result. Investors are the targets for an unbelievable barrage of messages from corporations seeking investment money. The "spin" training and the image-making methods deployed by political groups and corporations are the real forms of 1984 Orwellian platforms of "doublespeak" and manipulation. "Protect and preserve individual wants and needs at any cost is the essence of spin control," noted Sue Mackey, in a 1998 edition of *Washington CEO, Inc.* Spinning is a defensive measure. It is used to protect and keep things as they are. Spinners do not want to accept another message or hear another alternative. They already know as much as they want to know about any event, and they want you to join their belief. The postevent spin was demonstrated in the congressional hearings when Enron executives spun the tale about how little they knew and how innocent they were. We have no antivenom for investors to deal with this modern communications phenomenon. It is part of the information factories of corporations that manufacture truth or nontruth.

One of the great thin-air stories of Enron fame is how the board decided to alter the foundation for its actions. This is a curious way for a board to view its obligations to shareholders. Before the board participated in certain decisions, they wanted to ensure they did not violate the code of ethics. No problem. They suspended it. This is spinning and staying on message at its best. In this case they spun themselves into believing that they had done the right thing. They kept on repeating the idea until they accepted it as the best course of action, fully justified. This is how groups "norm" themselves into a behavior they think will get them where they need to get as a group. Then the board spun their newly justified message outside of the boardroom. On January 19, 2002, Reed Abelson reported in the *New York Times* that Enron's very prominent board had oversight of the special purpose entities and partnerships that led to Enron's downfall. At one point, the board went so far as to suspend its code of ethics in order to approve the creation of the special partnerships and the role that the Enron CFO would play in managing the partnerships. Waving the code somehow magically empowered the board to support a series of decisions that were not in the best interests of the share-holders. The board was fully informed yet decided to forget its code of ethics and its fiduciary responsibilities, therefore creating more risk for its shareholders.

The Enron case sheds light on how some boards value their codes of ethics. We now understand how executives can hit the moral switch and decide and declare that what they are doing and what they say they are doing is just fine. If a board with the credentials of the Enron members can operate in this manner, what shall we expect from the poorly constituted boards we see in so many corporations? We have found out that in the process of staying on message, the high-pressure conditions of our market cause messages to get corrupted. Trustees in a boardroom, with or without codes of ethics, and business leaders can lose control of messages and the truths they may have once contained.

Messages not subject to the interrogation of those investors with "skin in the game" are messages we should not trust at face value. Few things are worse than having a code of ethics that is totally ignored. One of them is treating the code as a trivial little piece of paper that can be turned on or off to fit the needs of the directors. This is the ultimate act of arrogance and disrespect for our system of laws and our views about what is right. When ethical foundations get in the way, waive them. If you are an investor, this situation should alert you to the need and the obligation to find out as much as you can about boards of directors. They are the ones behind the things corporations tell the public. These are the "officers of trust" who can, by their disregard for the public, create victims of corporate lies. These are the people most accountable when corporations go bad. Corporate leaders, and those who attend to them, must remember that loose talk of claims without factual foundations will cause problems. With any luck, investors will be looking at and listening to everything corporations say and report. Investors, now already more active than ever, will probably find more ways of challenging the overly optimistic claims or foundationless reports of irresponsible executives. For certain, no one will depend on annual reports and the old ways of presenting the "corporate story." Now we know these instruments of communication were declarations without foundation. They contained lies and were delivered through "spinning" machines and by people who stayed on message. Wouldn't it be refreshing to talk to someone who told it exactly as it was? How different it would be if we could ask a politician or businessperson a question and receive a direct, truthful answer. Truth be told, about half the time when you ask a CEO, "How is business?" the truthful answer would be, "It sucks." Ever heard that answer from a Fortune 500 CEO?

CHAPTER FIVE

The Fog of Corporate Complexity

The study of complex systems is about understanding indirect effects.

— From the MIT Conference on Complexity 2000

THE FUNDAMENTALS OF COMPLEXITY

Complexity is a formal academic discipline with a focus on complicated organizations such as corporations. The idea of complexity applies to organizations in large corporations where the business culture has become nearly impossible to describe or understand. Large complex organizations foster subgroups and small tribes where new behaviors emerge and many significant activities are hidden from normal view. This is the raw material for business anthropologists and organizational development experts. Complex human structures contain layers of relationships, power centers, and self-directed goals, which can move beyond the assigned or formal responsibilities of the group. Enron was such an organization. It was a global complex with hidden linkages within and without the formal organization. Enron, and hundreds of other companies, have used the complexity of their organizational structures with special covenants and rules to create thousands of partnerships and other formations for the express purpose of funneling money to the insider players. Enron officials deployed the organization for the purpose of creating unfair advantages and opportunities for a select few, by hiding large amounts of corporate debt, creating fake revenue, and arranging for hidden money to escape the shareholders' diligence. Deceptive complexity in organizations requires the innovative work of people, special norms and capabilities of communications, and the intent to commit the resources of the corporation in directions that are often inappropriate or illegal. In due course, complexity is difficult to control or understand as more activities are conducted out of the boundaries of normal managerial control. In time, corporations find that it is as difficult to find the real facts for themselves as it is to cover up facts they wish to hide.

Most people think they occupy the high ground when it comes to ethical business conduct. However, getting the facts right is a challenge. As we have observed and studied businesses over the years, we have found that finding the truth requires discipline. Often, companies find that they have produced a report with bad data, have described an event that is not exactly correct, or declared that something was true when it was not. With the very best of intentions, corporate leaders and managers get it wrong more often than we would guess. This condition is one of

the indirect effects of complexity in modern global businesses. Large modern corporations swim in a daily sea of
complexity. Their record keeping, data gathering, and
awareness of all the facts, figures, and details are challenged under the best of circumstances. Running a company with 200 locations around the world, 100,000
employees, and ten lines of business is bound to create a
complex business environment. Even companies much
smaller than this are filled with complexities. Yet we
expect and demand that the management team know what
is going on all the time in order to nail down the details
that affect market value.

Running a global corporation is like running a government. Thousands of events occur every day. Employees
die or are killed in accidents. Facilities are involved in
fires, floods, or explosions. Competitors attack in the
marketplace, and fortunes rise and fall in reaction to gov-
ernmental action, acts of nature, new contracts, and war.
Companies, in fact, know how to run themselves perhaps
with much greater efficiency than nations. They have
global structures and intelligent methods of monitoring
events in every country office and account around the
world. The push of global competition has added to the
complexity of day-to-day operations. Internet companies
developed thousands of alliances and partnerships to
make their business models unique and competitive.
Amazon.com has boasted about the thousands of alliances
they maintain to run their Internet business. It has one of
the most complex business models around for a company
that went through billions for years without showing a
profit. The Amazon story was all about "new economy"
models, innovative and complex alliance deals, and dif-

ferent ways of keeping the business scorecard. A lot of
investors bought this story. Some of them made money; a
lot of them lost money waiting for the story to come true.

Global companies often have more alliance partners
than employees. Alliances bring thousands of outside
people under the corporate tent, extending the already
complex business arrangements and new vulnerabilities.
This is a growing trend of "extended" complexity. Modern
corporations manage, or attempt to manage, thousands of
shifting and complex business relationships, each with its
own revenue, profit, and debt impacts on the value of the
company. The large pharmaceuticals manage 3,000 to
5,000 business alliances with drug testers, contract
researchers, consultants, and hospitals. This "collabora-
tive" business model is a real challenge to traditional
forms of oversight and governance. This is a permanent
trend of the global economy that will grow and become
even more complex. Alliances and partnership deals take
the form of equity-sharing business entities, holding companies, and the now-famous Enron-style "special purpose
entities." When these advanced business arrangements are
extended into global locations, the level of complexity is
multiplied. The unknowns in these business equations are
the new sources of business risk.

Enron used complexity to hide the facts about its
business. They created special purpose entities, more
than 2,000 of them, for the purpose of hiding debt and
manipulating the numbers they reported to Wall Street.
Partnerships, alliances, licensing agreements, subcon-
tracts, lease agreements, contracts, and financing methods are legitimate instruments of business. They are also
hiding places for business fraud. When auditors simply
look at the surface of the books, they are not likely to

understand how these tools of deception are being applied. The ways managers keep up with the facts of their companies and the ways auditors look at the books have fallen behind the new wave of organizational and administrative constructs developed by global businesses. There is a growing disconnection between the traditional ways of examining and measuring business reality and how reality takes shape today. A lot of the fundamentals are the same. However, in those areas that are different, the differences are just enough to be significant.

In the past few years businesses have gravitated to complex "supply chain" arrangements with each other. The supply chain concept dominates the operational activity of many large corporations. Supply chains require complex agreements about financial transactions and inventory management. The old ways of managing the logistics of business were complicated enough, but the new global supply chains are as complex as it gets. This is just one relatively new business structure that provides foggy complexity for hiding business problems. Investors will have a real challenge understanding how supply chains work. This discipline is managed by a new elite, often from the large consulting companies. These special experts run the strange world of supply chain, and they alone are the ones who really understand this strange world.

Business processes today, after more than a decade of reengineering, are still in bad shape for one major reason: The processes have focused on efficiency and speed, often at the expense of verification and accuracy. Perfectly good business leaders do not know everything they need to because they have not demanded that accuracy be the foundation of all business operations. During the period now known as "the Internet bubble," we developed bad habits such as "ballparking" the figures and trying to operate at the new speeds of business. We came up with all kinds of catchy slogans to describe our "power plays" and "speed to market" maneuvers. What we really did was forget about the ultimate responsibility and accountability we have for getting things right. Form overcame the substance of good business and correct operational details. As a result, big mistakes became visible, and the grand information repositories of business became suspect. The worst outcome of all was that we fooled ourselves into thinking we had great, innovative business practices. Enron thought they had it right. Over the next few years as complexity continues, the tolerance for getting off track will create greater risk for corporations and investors. A new level of vigilance is required.

Does the rise of complexity signal anything of great importance? One business analyst speaking about the weak players in the professional services industry noted that those with the weakest offerings and service capabilities depend on complex, fancy deal making to seduce their clients. What they and their clients eventually learn is that the deals are too complex to produce long-lasting value for either side. Clients lose faith in the vendors' ability to deliver, and vendors learn that they cannot make profit. They enjoy the glow of the first year or two and the public recognition for their genius deal making and large cash transfers. When the dust settles over the next five years, they learn they both lost. This is what we see in the complexity of business today.

Complexity may be a symptom of the rise of weak and unproven business models. Some say the real problem with Enron was that the business model did not work.

Every new organizational form, every seeming stretch into a new business area, added to the complexity of the company and lengthened the time required for business failure. According to some, complexity is a by-product of competing in global markets; it is an expression of business innovation. We do not think so. We believe that the trend toward more complexity is by and large what Enron made of it: a hiding place for greed and incompetence. It makes finding the truth more difficult and promotes a form of irresponsibility among executives who believe that it is okay for them not to know everything. This is the new excuse when things go wrong. The CEO of Enron and his wife both said it was impossible to know everything, ergo, they were not responsible. The question remains then: Who is?

TRUTH IS COMPLEX IN BUSINESS

Unless corporate leaders have really taken the steps to make sure that their corporate details are right and that their people are driven by the idea of truthful behavior, they cannot be sure about their own facts. Telling the truth, getting the facts right, and verifying the accuracy of important details are difficult tasks and major responsibilities. The CEO and the directors are responsible for making sure the corporation gets the facts right. There is no way out of this responsibility without giving up the executive or director role and letting someone who is responsible take on the job. Executives should not take on the executive mantle unless they know how to manage their fiduciary responsibilities to shareholders. We hope that everyone will underscore these very simple ideas one more time.

This notion of executive responsibility occurred to us with full force during several consulting engagements where we sat in on discussions between CEOs and CFOs about the numbers. In the act of probing for the details about "where are we on the numbers?" we heard various financial teams say, "We think we are on target here, but we have a drop-off in revenue, we think, in this unit that we cannot explain right now." A good example of this issue is in booking and reporting sales numbers. CFOs often receive a set of numbers from the sales teams on what has been booked. These numbers contain real sales, which have been completed. They may also contain "factored sales" numbers or probabilistic projections of sales that should come in soon. Under the pressures of making the numbers, the two kinds of sales get mixed together in a report. Then the sales teams get the order to "make sure those sales come in." Sometimes the CEO understands that he is looking at two different kinds of numbers, sometimes not. The fact is that the only sales that are real sales are the ones where customers have signed agreements. Even then, a percentage of signed deals fall apart. What is the truth about sales? Take your choice.

To illustrate the point further, this time in a political context, David Murray (The Statistical Analytic Services Group website) points out that "the illusion of certainty is Washington's stock in trade. There are no real numbers in Washington. There are only useful numbers and nonuseful numbers." Congressional members, like their executive counterparts in business, must make use of numbers. They too make choices. These conversations take place every day. Financial officers and their teams struggle to make sure they have the right facts. What they eventually discover is that the orientation toward accuracy and candor is a cultural factor. It is not invented overnight or directed to come into existence. Creating a culture with the right orientation requires leadership from the top and work by the entire company. You do not turn it on and off. Your business culture is either based on candor and honesty or it is not. There is no middle ground of dependability. Whatever the cultural norms, speed and fast growth will change the culture. The Enron culture was driven by innovation, smart people, and big ideas on the one hand and twisted by financial engineering and greed on the other. As we've learned, these do not go together. But, the question is, how does a company keep them apart?

This issue of "organizational or cultural legitimacy" is another section of the complexity chain. Corporations create strategies, structures, and cultures, which accept their modes of operating and defend the work of the corporation. In global companies, organizational complexity allows the executives to deploy the politics of the executive suite to make sure they always have a cadre of loyal soldiers to help get things done. While the culture of each different business unit may have its own way of operating, there is always someone around with the right connections to the top to ensure the big decision makers know what is going on and can move the organization in the direction they want. Inside the organizations, team leaders and loyal workers are inundated with motivational messages about the work they do and the progress of the corporation. They come to accept and believe what they hear and do what they are asked to do. The close insiders may have a different perspective on what is going on in the company, but most of them are already co-opted by their positions, stock, or other factors. These organizational dynamics allow the company to manage programs of mendacity that cut through global operations. This management work is complex and confusing even for those who manage it. CEOs understand their organizations very well, and they know how to move the organization. Executive recruiters are reminded repeatedly by search committees of the board to find leaders who are "organizationally savvy," who know how to maneuver through the politics of large organizations and get things done. This is a core competence of the modern executive. They know how to move the organization and find out what is going on. It is the key to their survival and one of the primal instincts of the CEO. While they do create complexity, never let them tell you that they do not know what is going on. True, they do not know every detail. This was the defense of Enron leaders and others who continually appeared before Congress. But they do know what is going on with the big numbers and the big deals. Complaining about not knowing all the details is just an act of hiding behind complexity.

As the quarterly conference call date with Wall Street analysts approaches, the scramble to get the details out of the organization and produce stories for the public moves into high gear. "Where are we, where are we trending, are we making the forecast, how can we explain our situation, and how will the analysts react?" This is the normal string of questions from the CEO and a few directors. They already have a good feel for what they may need to do or say. CEOs and CFOs always have the big picture and the superior information about where things really are, but they want to make sure they do not trip over an obvious fact they have forgotten. They also depend on the troops to gather the data from the usual places. We have participated, as observers, on these calls and have witnessed interesting situations. This is a critical process of fact gathering. The best companies conduct it in an open and rigorous environment where every fact is treated with care. The unethical leaders already know what they want to do with the facts, and they conduct a session of pretense and manipulation. Their focus is on earnings and stock management for personal gain. This focus takes them away from operational details and strategic management issues. This is why they often claim they did not know what was going on at one level. But they always know where the money is. The former Enron CEO told Congress that he did not know about the details of the special partnerships and the detailed financial arrangements. Twenty-four hours later his former office manager revealed that he led the meeting for the partnerships and was deeply into the facts. Investors, from now on, will want to understand more about how corporate leaders know what they know and how they know it. This is the big area of executive competence and managerial skill. Investors want to validate that business leaders have the competence and know-how to manage, even in complexity. The Enron executive gang was not collectively dumber than a bag of hammers. They just lacked the competence and candor to produce shareholder value.

Without reference to the facts he knew to be right, one CEO took to the phone and announced, "We clearly see the markets moving down, but our industry is immune to these particular cycles. Our top-level work is always in demand. In fact, these markets typically create more opportunities for us. And, as for the next quarter, we will be right on target." He was dead wrong, even though he said he was telling the truth. Why did this CEO get it wrong when he could have gotten it right? Like the captain of the *Titanic,* everything he knew was wrong. His was a case of incompetence compounded by a reactive stretching of the facts he knew. He was hoping against hope that his story would allow the market to give him more time to make his story come true. Like so many CEOs in the high-pressure seat of leadership, he did not take the time to find and verify the real facts. His ego told him he was the leading expert on how the world really worked. The typical leader under the pressures of keeping his publicly traded company on target will say a lot of things that are not true. They do so because they lack a solid process for validating the accuracy of what they say to analysts, investors, and the business press. Or they say the wrong thing because they want to manipulate the stock or get around poor performance. Under the pressures of appearing to be on track, particularly in the area of revenue recognition, they look for ways to make the numbers come true. The pressures are so great and the appearance of failure so high, they cannot see other choices.

First, to get to the truth, you must have a "reality" orientation. This means a process and a managerial focus on maintaining situational awareness. The old fundamentals of having a realistic perspective about the markets are a good place to start. We heard a lot of strange logic in some of the conference calls and business plans we studied. People actually say and believe, "The market we are in will be at $20 billion, growing at 20 percent each year, within the next five years, and we are strongly positioned to grow with the markets. Therefore, we will hit our revenue target of $200 million next quarter." This logic, even by the person who says it, really requires some validation.

As most of the Internet jockeys found out last year, the potential existence of a strong and growing market actually means very little in terms of what you will do in your business. Getting a realistic grip on what you can reasonably do in a market is the first of the forgotten duties of business leaders. If the processes by which companies produce their business plan, market estimates, and forecasts are flawed at the outset, the die is cast for getting trapped by unrealistic, invalidated, and overly optimistic views about business opportunities. We have just come from a period when this practice was the norm—a period in which most companies developed some very bad habits. Complexity enters the equation in this area as well. Since there is so much inflated data about business performance, it is now nearly impossible to get to a detailed level of understanding about market data. Various business units will use a variety of methods and assumptions in the study of their data. They will produce plans and forecasts that are not accurate in critical ways. These plans get accepted and written down in corporate reports and public documents as if they were absolute laws. The inaccuracy and sloppiness feeds on itself around a wide circle of global business data. This is the stuff reports are made of and on which people depend to make informed decisions. It is data that is almost correct and causes almost-correct decisions. Market research resides in so many forms and in so many conflicting viewpoints that you can make your market data come out the way you want it. Like the pro forma report on performance projections, marketing plans have drifted far away from the realism of how strong the markets really are and what companies can really do.

Part of the reality-based management companies

should get back to is the use of the "rude" question. In the introduction of this book we gave you a feel for the kind of rude questions investors should ask companies. Inside the company, *performance reality* demands first and foremost intellectual honesty. Tom Clancy, in his 1992 novel *Sum of All Fears,* reminds us that "the mark of intellectual honesty is the solicitation of opposing points of view." Managers around the decision table should ask a few of these questions about every report, action, or decision that could impact the company: How do we know this information is absolutely accurate? How do we verify our data and reports? What are the alternative points of view on the information used to make our decisions? What are the unintended consequences of our decisions? What will this course of action do for our shareholders? What are the risks to the company and shareholders? What questions should we be asking ourselves that we have failed to ask?

Uncertainty abounds in corporations, and it may not always be possible to assure total accuracy. Many of the biggest and best decisions are made in the fog of uncertainty by leaders with sound judgment. Those who lie are not concerned about knowing all they need to know about a decision. They are blinded by their single-minded focus for more money and more power.

Questions need to be asked and verifiable answers need to be produced. When companies tell us how they are going to dominate the markets, we need to know more. So do they.

Telling the truth about what you plan to do in markets is one thing; telling the truth about your actual abilities to sustain the effort over time is another. A lot of things must come together for a company to hit its targets. Few leaders want to talk about all the planets they must align to get the results they promised. Although this is the real work of business leadership, analysts are not very interested in the realities of the workplace. They just want you to tell them that you are going to make it. The story becomes less interesting if they hear about all the things you must do. There were thousands of business failures in 2000. Most of them were Internet start-ups. There were thousands more in 2001. The variety of company types expanded in that year. All of them shared something in common. Their beliefs about the strength of the markets and the market share that they would capture for their shareholders were all wrong. The facts were not correct. They never were.

Telling the truth in hard times has its own special demands. When the curves are moving down the chart, there seems to be added pressure to explain them away as if they were not true or not important. We have seen case after case where CEOs told the street that the trend lines did not apply to them; they were experiencing a small bump in the road that would have no impact on the long term. Ken Lay, who once again took over as CEO of Enron when Jeffrey Skilling resigned, issued a press release on August 14, 2001, announcing the resignation. In that release, Ken Lay said, "Our business is extremely strong and our growth prospects have never been better." In a later speech to employees, October 23, 2001, when the company was going under, there were several hostile questions. One of them was "I would like to know if you are on crack? If so, that would explain a lot; if not, you may want to start because it's going to be a long time before we trust you again." This was an emotional question from an employee clearly angered by Ken Lay's casual demeanor.

Investors are likely to become more interested in the processes by which companies ensure the accuracy of what they say about markets, revenues, profits, and performance. The sound bite approach to understanding company information does not work. Investors are no longer interested in stories. They want to know if the company has the integrity to get anything right.

COMPLEXITY IN THE INFORMATION EXCHANGE

Large transnational organizations are complicated in every way and operate in an intricate maze of business transactions. It's a perfect place to be inventive with information. It is also an interesting environment with complex "information exchanges" that contribute to the difficult task of finding the truth. One of the first and most powerful illusions where information is exchanged is in the business press and the associated business media channels. Investors can tune in to the business channels and light up their eyes with colorful electronic tickers, graphs, and charts by the thousands, and neat columns and rows of figures that create the appearance of dead-on precise calculated truth. It's not true. At best, the data that companies report and media pick up are rounded estimates and best guesses of where things are. Balance sheets can always be made to balance within the rules. Off the balance sheet, information can always be kept so far off the audit trails as to be hidden from view. Reports, based on certain assumptions and the application of the right rules, can come out to what you need them to be at the time. They do not always represent the precision that is impressed upon you by your broker's charts and the reporters' spreadsheets. This information is just good enough to pass muster. It is the land of "almost right" but not exactly right. That is how Enron can have great charts and favorable analyst comments one week and six weeks later fall off the edge. The "chartists" rely on data that range from 98 percent correct to 99 percent wrong. How can you possibly figure out when the numbers are right or wrong? As an individual investor, you probably cannot. You are left to play the odds by placing your trust in a broker, a friend, or by following the herd. Blackjack is much easier. The card dealer will at least tell you how the game is played. We do not exactly get the same level of candor when we rely on the information provided in the great information exchanges on television and in the business press.

During the week of January 28, 2002, as the Enron situation continued to unwind, the market suddenly dropped by over 200 points in the middle of the week. For two days the financial television channels talked for hours about the loss of investor confidence in the markets. "Enronitis," according to the reporters, was causing investors to back away from the market. They reported on the crisis of confidence and mused about what it would take to set things right. The Tyco Corporation saw its stock fall and said it was unfair. The street was asking about Tyco accounting practices, the restructuring of the company, and the fact that the top executives had sold a lot of stock. The investing public was looking through the Enron lens at market action. It did not help that during that week, the SEC directly challenged company accounting practices in several other cases. The SEC warned several banks about their aggressive accounting practices.

During this chaos, a series of interviews was conducted by CNN to examine market confidence. One institutional investor noted that as close as they could get inside companies, even as professional investors, they could not be sure of the numbers they saw. Ron Insana, of CNBC news, interviewed a lot of people on this topic. Nearly everyone agreed that it was no longer possible to find the facts. What they did not say was that they were going to report the facts anyway. As soon as the interviews were over, it was back to the charts and graphs. Professional investors had just said it was hard to get the numbers. In the next few minutes these investors were reporting numbers, picking stocks, and pushing the market as they always had. They had also called for reform and said this time we will get the reforms done. But it was life as usual on the TV. It's a profitable format, and no one wants that to change.

We have a business media, stock analysts posing as journalists, and CEOs who want to make money, gathered in a silent confirmation that it is a good thing to meet on the financial channels and suggest what investors should do. It is okay for them to talk up the stocks when they cannot verify the numbers or if they have a conflict of interest. If the financial channels did not interview people with conflicts of interest, they would have few interviews. Those with firm objective viewpoints and no conflicts of interest provide far too sober assessments of corporations.

During the summer of 2001, Congress held hearings on the subject of stock analysts with potentially serious conflicts of interest. The acting chairperson of the SEC, Laura S. Unger, testified along with representatives from the financial press. All expressed concern over the fact that analysts, investment bankers, stock research organizations, and the financial media had come together to pump up stocks. The financial press news stations were particularly aggressive in providing the platform for stocks to be hyped on a daily basis, according to those who testified. When confronted with this issue some months after the hearings, one of the officials from CNBC noted, in a separate interview, "There is no such thing as unbiased information from Wall Street." His attitude was that people who listen to the financial news should know better than to believe all of what they hear. CNN, CNBC, Bloomberg, and others in financial radio and television seem to be of one mind on this point. There are no warning labels on the bad information one receives from Wall Street, from whatever source, and there is no validation that the good information is good. Investors are on their own. The attitude of so many of the producers and spreaders of corporate information is that bad data are all over the place, and you, the receivers of information, better beware. If you are not sure about the information you get, do not buy stocks. You must find your own truth in the markets; no one is going to provide it for you.

It became clear during the SEC hearings in the summer of 2001 that investment bankers and research organizations that had an interest in certain stocks used the business press to pump up their own financial interests. At the same time, the analysts and financial pundits on financial news networks presented themselves as objective advisers or experts. While CNBC executives may have suggested that there is no unbiased information on Wall Street, these media folks created the image of highly skilled, very bright, scientifically objective analysts who had the real information about the best stocks. Sometimes they do. Rarely does anyone look back on their record based on sound-bite recommendations during a television interview. Often the hyped stocks had terrible records and poor values. In a few instances they pushed companies already under investigation for significant illegalities. They did not feel the need to present all the facts on hand—just the facts that made the stock look good. In this context, the business media became "Enroned." That is, they unwittingly or otherwise participated in presenting a false picture of stock values. Financial newscasters have changed their behavior, at least on the surface, since Enron. We have noticed that they are becoming more careful with the facts. They have even started asking questions about conflicts of interest. We hope this trend continues. Several journalism awards have been presented to newspapers for their coverage of Enron and related fraud cases. This is an improvement, not the solution. Annual reports, conference calls, and business media reports appear to be of the same pedigree. They are extensions of each other and parts of the great business information exchange that is capable of providing reports that are almost true or dead wrong. You have to figure it out. What we see is an enthusiastic business media in close, often cozy, relationships with business leaders. They ask a few hard questions but are primarily accommodating and supportive of "Wall Street," who buys most of their advertising and provides most of their guests. What we do not see is a persistent counterpoint press or the accommodation of critics of the process. We are getting the equivalent of a one-note song.

The 2001 hearings about the business media and conflicts of interest produced no action. Congressional leaders said they feared the coming of widespread fraud unless the conditions were improved to prevent such blatant conflicts of interest among the business media, investment bankers, and corporations. They also noted that policing all of this kind of activity was beyond the capabilities of the SEC to handle. Yet Congress does not want to take on the role of policing this activity. They much prefer, as Wall Street does, to have the industry police itself. The Enron case will not let Congress get away without taking some action. Hundreds of bills are in the pipeline that will be in debate in 2002. This is the problem. The debates will take forever. What on the surface appears as the most congressional action we have seen on this topic will fade in never-ending debates. No doubt, Congress will pass a few rules and make some changes. We believe that they will force some real action in the area of conflict of interest among analysts. They may even help the SEC get on track in the work of enforcement. But they will not take on the press or financial TV. The press is the press. They have the First Amendment with them at all times, and properly so. The press will police itself if there is enough pressure or concern. Independent members of the financial press have now gone on record to point out that there is a real problem in the age of instant financial information and in preventing the fast flow of false information. Audited data as well as the homespun pro forma data are instantly available on the Internet or on the SEC Edgar site. People move this information around, package it, and repeat it, not knowing if it is correct. They can expose bad information to millions of people in just a few seconds. MSNBC, CNN, CNBC and financial Webcasters pick up the information and send it around the world without any warning labels.

Good data and lies occupy the same set of electrons as they move around the world at the speed of light. This is a different world where, in this case, the enforcement infrastructure has a fraction of the impact of rogue financial information and those who produce it by accident or otherwise. What is most difficult about our business culture at this point in history is the power of technology to amplify information around the world instantly. Business leaders and their Wall Street backers already have a press platform that is unmatched in business history. They now use the power of the Internet and of their executive positions to spread their version of the truth. Far too many times "their version" is not true, not fully disclosed, and not free of conflicts of interest.

Wall Street analysts have become pseudo-celebrities. The news networks are owned in most cases by larger corporations that have viewpoints on financial matters. It is not easy to report all the facts as a reporter when your parent corporation has interests at stake. Professional investors now pretend to be objective journalists, investors, and commentators. These things do not go together according to Christopher Byron of *High Noon on Wall Street.* Byron, who testified in the summer hearings, went on to say that there has been a riot in the pursuit of money. IPOs were offered to banks, and the banks pumped up demand through their analysts and reporting. This behavior created billion-dollar events that burst finally in the so-called Internet crash of the past two years. This is fraud on a new scale according to Byron. In January 2002, a *Frontline* episode provided detailed documentation about the apparent corruption and control of the entire IPO process by the investment bankers of Wall Street. This documentary revealed how the bankers control IPOs, and how they determine who is included or excluded in stock allocations. This report paints the picture of the very front end of the market process that is just as hidden and mysterious as revenue reporting. IPOs are the beginning of the information exchange with the public. The "road shows" and the press hype about new offerings bring together, usually for the first time, the corporate insiders, bankers, market makers, analysts, and the press. This is where the relationships begin and continue long into the market. If this basic market development process continues to be conducted half underneath the table and half without good facts, the rest of the process will never get better. The IPO process needs as much reform as any accounting or revenue processes. They are all concentrations or with-holding points of vast information that investors must get right. However, no one inside the IPO process today wants change.

Business leaders, like many of their financial jour-nalist friends, are part of the business celebrity move-ment. CEOs often act like rock stars during interviews with the financial media. Tradeshows attract the big CEOs and feature them in elaborate staged presentations with music and floodlights.

It is show biz for business. CEOs are a part of the story and the packaging effort to pump up the stock at IPO or at any time. They give their reports, increasingly based on the pro forma method (the make-it-up-as-you-go-along method of reporting company performance): The news is passed on by the reporter during live broad-casts, brokers push their picks of the week, the stock goes up, and the insiders cash in before the real data can be found out. This chain of capital manipulation has been perfected over the past few years and is not likely to go away quickly. There is too much money to be made. There has also been too much good news. Today, however, there is not a lot of good news about markets. But, in boom times, good news is all you get. Only 1 percent of broker recommendations tell you to sell, and the potential is even lower in the category of "strong sell." Even during a one-year slide downward of the market, the hipsters on the financial broadcasts were not telling anyone to sell anything. They promoted stocks to buy and often promoted companies that were already on the edge. When they push a stock, they use an arcane language that can mean what they want it to mean, nothing more or nothing less. There is no common scale in the language of recommendations. You can listen to five slightly different views on a stock and come away with the belief that the stock is a buy. In reality, it could be a sell. There needs to be a decoder for this jargon and a realist who can help investors make sense of this. Of course, if this were possible, companies might be more careful in managing performance information. For now, corporations can hide behind the information exchanges conducted in the public financial media. It is the perfect place to be creative with information. Recognition through press coverage is a form of currency among the marketing staff of corporations. They compile press clippings each week and report to the CEO, "See, we are in the press in a favorable light." A brighter light might reveal that the favor is misplaced. There are plenty of gaps in the information. First, the public needs to know the historical recommendation data, data that are now locked up. It takes more effort and time than most of us have to find out this information.

It would be interesting if investment banks were to disclose their historical underwriting relationships, for these are the very trails that are the most difficult to unearth. Who could possibly uncover all the permutations of conflicts of interest between all the players and producers of investment information? Today no one is responsible for this, and no one is really capable of finding out. We depend on disclosure, and disclosure alone does not work. What is not working today is disclosures of the interest of all the parties engaged in investment activity. Pre-IPO details and IPO details are not transparent and hide a number of inside deals. The IPO is controlled through the power of allocation decisions that investors do not know about. In many investment turning points, material omissions prevent an understanding of deal structures and who holds what kind of interest in the deals. Conflicts of interest arise through the continuous complexity of financial arrangements in the life cycle of corporations. For disclosure to have value, it would need to be more complete around these events:

Critical Disclosure Event

- Just before the IPO; Road Show and pre-IPO publicity
- The first year of post-IPO performance results and changes
- During mergers or acquisitions: accounting details
- During an SEC inquiry
- During bankruptcy
- During small market corrections downward
- During large market corrections upward
- During any performance reporting including audits
- During shareholder meetings
- During stock picks and promotions by financial TV

These are the prime times when corporate leaders and investor relations teams get creative with information or fail to present all the facts. These events significantly and materially shift the value of corporations, or may do so, in ways that prevent investors from tracking the net results. Anna Chason, from the National Association of Real Estate Investment Trust, says, "Investor relations have been described as a fencing match conducted on a tightrope. In providing information to investors and analysts, corporate officers must carefully negotiate the 'high wire' and provide full information while avoiding 'selective disclosures' or disclosures of material non-public information to a select group rather to the market as a whole." Regulation Fair Disclosure requires, but does not yet obtain, the "fullness" investors require. Corporations have protected reserves of details that regulations have not uncovered yet through rules or enforcement. It takes a long time to figure out what was said, if was true, if it was a lie, if it was a typo, or if it was a conspiracy. If it was a lie, it takes a long time to sort out the details and determine who did what. If you do get caught, in most cases, not much will happen. If I steal your $50,000 car and get caught, I could go to jail for grand theft auto. If I cheat you out of the value of $2 million of your shares, I could get off with just a little bad press. In our short-term-memory culture, we all move on and forget—except those who are left holding an empty bag that once contained a lot of stock value. This is the function of the information exchange. The information exchange process allows for the management of time and messages so that corporations can create the perceptions they need to keep investors in the market before bad news or the truth has an impact. This kind of manipulative exchange makes things look better than they are. Beyond the free flow of information from corporations and through the media, there are others who add to the "not-exactly-true" stories we hear about corporations, their stock, and their performance.

SURROGATES IN THE SERVICE OF LIES

Why should a company lie when it can pay others to do it? Some companies need to do both. They clearly need the services of others to spread their messages whether they are true or false. This is the fundamental method of saturating the market with your message. The complexity of the corporation extends in all of its acts of communications and through these mechanisms spread across financial institutions. Professional communications programs are an important means for the propagation of complexity and the messages that cause investors to act without accurate information. That is where the surrogates, the public relations and advertising firms, come in. These "messaging" professionals accept a fee to get out your message, whatever it is. These are the firms that develop hard-hitting and often personally targeted messages during political campaigns. The Andersen auditors, for example, have taken out full-page advertisements in the largest newspapers to saturate the nation with its defensive message about working for Enron. Their communications engines are running at full rpm to persuade us all that Andersen is a great company. They have cranked up their lobby teams, and perhaps their political contributions, to get the messages out. These events were covered in various financial TV reports.

If we characterize this process in the worse possible way, we would call it propaganda. Investors must decide, from their own wisdom, if they are staring into the barrel of a daily barrage of propaganda designed to manipulate and persuade rather than enlighten and inform. In our experience the propaganda label fits well enough that investors should assume a very critical attitude about what they hear. It is what they do not tell you that makes propagandists dangerous. It does not matter if surrogate communicators attack the good character of a political opponent and float a story that is not true or at best pitifully distorted. They have a job to do, and they do it well. Public relations and advertising firms have been blamed for many things. They are painted as the evil geniuses who come up with the political smear ad campaigns, for selling the Gulf War to save Kuwait to the American people, for promoting dangerous products, and for helping companies get out of trouble when things go wrong by creating false or deceptive image-building campaigns. They also promote stories and ideas that are true. They can educate, condition, or mislead on a global scale. They are the professional storytellers.

During the past fifteen years there has been a major consolidation of the large PR and advertising firms with two or three very large, global firms that work for the Fortune 500 corporations. These "communications services" giants provide integrated communications, imaging and messaging services for large corporations. They support investor-relations programs and help with the annual reports and all printed materials a corporation may need to get its messages out. These companies will create a story or an entire communications campaign aimed at particular public audiences in an effort to persuade. Part of the value of the consulting services they provide is in the area of integrating and coordinating the communications of global corporations. They have the information methodologies and tools to take quick polls to find out what people hope and what they will believe. They use this real-time information to craft messages for their corporate and political clients.

They make sure that a consistent and regular message arrives on target with great frequency. They know how to measure the impact of their programs, and they know when to use which techniques. During the 1980s, an executive at J. Walter Thompson went on record in *PR Watch* to explain how these companies view their own capabilities: "We have within our hands the greatest aggregate means of mass education and persuasion the world has ever seen—namely, the channels of advertising communication. We have power. Why do we not use it?"* Since the 1980s we have seen these professionals not only use their power, but nearly perfect its use in political and corporate information campaigns.

The two biggest PR firms, WPP and Omnicon, were founded within a year of each other in the mid-1980s. Hill & Knowlton and Burson-Marsteller are now owned by the WPP group. WPP is known as the world's leading communications services group. Clients of the WPP group include most of the Fortune Global 500 and the NASDAQ 100. The WPP group, with all its units, has a total market value of more than $14 billion. They have over 50,000 employees, in ninety-two countries, and have 1,300 offices. WPP controls more than eighty companies and provides services in branding and identity, demographic marketing, direction, promotion and relationship marketing, investor relations, public relations, strategic marketing consulting, and media investment and services. These companies are the creators and sustainers of cor-

---

*From *PR Watch,* Volume 8, No. 2.

porate messages. If the corporate message is true and important, they can drive it home and make sure it reaches the right audience and achieves the best effect. If the message is a lie, they can do the same.

This does not come as shocking news to any of us. We appreciate, in many cases, the superb work of the large PR firms in educating the public on a large scale. In fact, this is the issue, scale. These firms and the media technologies they employ are generating persistent messages on an unprecedented scale. They can impact the globe and make people believe their messages. If the messages are true and accurate, it is one thing. If the global messages are false, it is another. Corporations need this kind of professional assistance to get their messages across whatever the message is. It is impossible to reach the global public without them, but with them the potential for falsehood delivered on a grand scale is certain. Accountability for this emerging new global capability is not assured in ways to protect people from the false messages they may receive. When corporations use the large PR firms to affect the actions of investors, they have entered into a new realm of accountability and responsibility. They have become key players in the supply chain of information that impacts global markets. PR firms can become the unwitting conduit of corporate lies without knowing the role they have played.

This is an interesting area for research and one that probably needs more work. For example, it would be interesting to study the filings of a company in the middle of a complex and perhaps not-so-legal activity and then analyze what the PR and advertising messages were focusing on. We did see a little of this work in retrospect during the tobacco court cases. While the tobacco firms were swearing to the Congress that they did not believe nicotine was addictive in any way, and while they were hiding the research that proved that it was addictive, they hired PR firms to focus on the good things tobacco companies did for America. Even today, we see major advertising campaigns about the good works of big tobacco while they plan their product campaigns in Asia and other places where the social reaction to the health hazards of cigarettes has not yet caused any trouble for the corporations.

All of the large corporations pay fees for PR and advertising. Enron had their help in advertising and in the creation of its annual report. On the one hand, Enron used PR to tell things that were not true in both its annual report and press release. Their messages, whether true or false, can get to the markets if you have the money to pay the professionals and use their global reach. Executives want to build great brands and improve the "image" of their corporations. This is legitimate work. There are great brands, good products, and they deserve to be promoted. We are glad we have been informed about these companies and their products. On the other hand, corporations pay for advertising where there is little factual connection between the "image" and the actual day-to-day work of the company. The image is the target condition the corporation would like for you to believe they have already achieved. The facts are always different from the manufactured image. Consider the label on some car mirrors that says, "Objects appear smaller than they are." This is not too far off from the kind of warning label some of the image campaigns should have. In these cases the warning would be "The corporation appears more capable than it is."

The PR firms, advertising groups, and related consultants work together, particularly when a company is in crisis. When Texaco had a problem involving race discrimination a few years ago, it tried to fix the problem and fix the image. When companies are caught in shareholder lawsuits or SEC investigations, you will see them turn up the heat on the PR engine. When there has been a scandal in the company, the consultants are paid to work the problem and get the incident out of the news. They want to provide the positive news, the positive spin, and push any bad news off the table. They know as much about the "news cycle" as the politicians because this is what they get paid to do. Would you need a PR firm at all if your news was pretty good most of the time? You bet. They can help promote good news and really deliver an impact. They can create a stream of press releases, most of which will be accepted and unedited by the press.

According to Alex Carey in a May 1999 edition of the *Monitor,* "The twentieth century has been characterized by three developments of great political importance: the growth of democracy, the growth of corporate power, and the growth of corporate propaganda as a means of protecting corporate power against democracy." Forty percent of all news flows virtually unedited through public relations offices that are managing the perceptions of readers. This is the domain of the communications experts who know how to deliver the information their clients want you to see and to keep you distracted from information that clients do not want you to know about. If you do know about such information, they will quickly provide a spin or distortion, or a perspective that takes your attention in another direction. When the spin game is in full play, communications experts are not responsible for providing accurate, verified facts on both sides of a story. We would like to believe they give us the full story. But they have a "message" to get out, and they will do what it takes to get the message out and make sure it has been received and believed by the target audience. Corporations would probably be accused of not protecting shareholder value if they did not take advantage of competitive communications and use the experts to help them. The problem is that they very easily cross the lines between facts and fictions when they do so, and they pay PR firms to help them.

On May 15, 2001, the Federal Trade Commission settled a case involving charges of deceptive advertising against Gateway and Juno that pertained to the two companies' Internet access services. Consumers were promised free Internet access through an advertising campaign designed and developed by an advertising firm. The real story is that you had to use at least 150 free hours within one month. Cancellations were handled by a single, unpublished telephone number. Gateway customers were charged $3.95 per hour to use what was advertised as a toll-free number. Gateway made a few refunds but otherwise did not think any harm or false information had been presented. This is one among thousands of little settlements or warnings about deceptive advertising. These cases develop when the public complains about false advertising or inappropriate marketing practices. However, for the most part, people do not complain to the SEC or other agencies when corporate performance and images have been manipulated through public relations campaigns.

During the past year, a few watchdog agencies have complained about over-the-counter drug advertising. People are spending more on drugs these days, and it's not just because the prices of drugs are high. Some believe it is due to the fact that the big pharmaceuticals have spent millions promoting over-the-counter and prescription drugs directly to consumers through television advertising. During commercial breaks it is now possible to see up to three or four advertisements for drugs, one right behind the other. The opponents of these drug campaigns are trying to prove that this causes people to buy drugs they do not need. It causes them, some think, to ask their doctors for drugs that may not be right for them. We saw in the aftermath of the anthrax scare of 2001 that doctors will write prescriptions for the drugs for which people ask. Are the drug companies lying to the public about this? We do not know at this point. For now we are still digesting the messages that have been manufactured for our consumption. We do know that this is a very aggressive campaign on the part of the drug makers. From our experiences of the past, such aggressive selling probably has some built-in dangers. We just do not know what they are at this time. We wonder if the drug companies do. We also wonder why they do not tell us more about why they are pushing all of these drugs over our TV set. While it may be, in part, for the good health of the nation, they clearly have a product to sell, and TV is a good way to move product.

PR campaigns are an uncontrolled and powerful arena where corporations provide a one-way channel of information that is not often challenged. There is no Q&A after you have been bombarded with hundreds of advertisements. The PR campaigns around publicly traded corporations deserve the utmost skepticism from the investment community. With any luck, investors will be taking closer looks and listening harder when the PR blitz begins.

Powerful interest groups guard the work of the large public relations firms. After all, these are the firms' politicians, and business leaders rely on them for successful campaigns of all kinds. This is First Amendment territory. No one is prepared to intervene in any way in their work or to study the consequences of what they do with their messaging and imaging programs. There are a few critics, such as *PR Watch,* but by and large, the communications experts hired by the corporations have the freedom they need to do their work. No one knows better how to lobby Congress for what they want than the big PR firms. Next time you see the big corporate advertisement or read the big flashy annual report, remember that the producers of this information are not working for you. They are working for someone else who may or may not have your interests at heart. In fact, it is possible that they want to manage the difference between what they know and what they want you to believe.

MINDING THE GAP

During 2001 three Americans won the Nobel Prize in economics for their work in an area called "information economics." The big theory in their research has to do with "asymmetric information." The asymmetry of information always favors the seller of goods. Sellers always know more than buyers and can push market value with the superiority of information. They use market research to know more about the people to whom they sell than those people can know about the products or services they purchase.

The economists have uncovered an important fact about finding the truth in business dealings. Sellers of products and services create more short-term value for themselves broadening the information gap between themselves and their customers. However, over time, this practice leads to market breakdowns as customers learn not to trust the sellers and to offer no more than the average price of products sold in a certain category. This phenomenon of information asymmetry presents its symptoms in the strange rituals of conference calls, annual reports, and reports of audit. Companies do not want to provide so much information that buyers will have a reason to withdraw from their markets. Thus, they invent ways of talking about the financial status of the business, the numbers, and the future possibilities as ways to convince buyers to stay in the market. They are providing signals, without providing the details of what is really going on. In some cases the signals are correct or nearly correct. In an increasing number of cases the signals are not even close to any kind of reality. The traditional signaling system has become corrupt. As a result, at least in the capital markets, traditional and fuzzy signals will no longer suffice. Investors are already on the verge of demanding the real facts and closing the information gap.

What the Nobel Prize winners found is what we have all found: Disclosure is not a bad thing. Companies complain that they are suffering disclosure overload, or that more disclosure does not get to the reality of their unique situations. Most of them want to suggest that their business is unique and complex and requires a special kind of reporting and analysis, which only they and their special tea-leaf readers can understand. We would bet that there is not a company in North America that Warren Buffett could not figure out in about two hours at most. Companies need to disclose more details in a timely manner if they are interested in closing the information gap with those who invest in them. Off-balance-sheet details as well as accurate on-balance-sheet information are a minimum. Companies should be willing to provide certain information and certify that it is correct. The CEO, the CFO, and a few others should be willing to provide certification about the facts they provide as truth.

Some of the new rules under consideration for audit committees will require that the board members who oversee the audit teams must, in fact, "sign off" that the work is accurate. This will probably not solve the information gap problem. It may only cause directors to avoid service on audit committees. Somewhere along the way, corporations will need to ensure the accuracy of what the company is doing. In so many cases when companies have been found to lie about expenses, debt, and revenue, we see the CEO and the board appearing to be confused. They say they did not know. Analysts say they did not know and would have never guessed that the company was producing false reports. Someone always knows what is going on. In the future, the executive management team will not have the luxury of pretending to have been fooled by the CFO or the auditors.

The core of the issue is that complexity is used to hide the truth. It is quite amazing once you look at what has happened to our business culture. Businesses and their lobby groups have spent years and tens of millions of dollars to protect themselves from legislative measures they did not like. Instead, they have supported the evolution of a confusing kludge of rules, practices, and intertwined conflicts of interest that are undermining their prospects for long-term success in global markets. This maze of complexity is now in the process of being disowned by a few and seriously challenged by lawmakers. The entrenchment of the business community, their auditors, and their less-than-objective reporting is in the same fix as our Congress and campaign finance reform. We all hope for some movement in both of these cases. These are the areas where we believe progress will be made and solutions found.

- Accurate and verified communications: Corporations should show the world, and take pride in, their ability to produce accurate facts for investors.
- Full disclosure on conflicts of interest: This one is simple—if you have a conflict, declare it now.
- Real-time accounting and real-time reporting: The SEC is calling for closing the gap between when insiders sell and when they report what they have done. Technology, and a tighter time cycle, will help in reporting events.
- Straightforward accounting rules: Reduce the number of rules by 30 percent for starters, make them simple, and close the loopholes.
- Real accountability by executives: No more excuses about not knowing what was going on. If you cannot keep up, get out of the boardroom and turn in your options.

These areas of focus would begin to create the kinds of investor protection referred to in the first part of this book and help unravel the unnecessary and unproductive complexity of our business operations. For example, simple rules can be written to guide most corporate report-

ing. Auditors and companies would like for us to believe
that this is impossible. Every company requires a special
way to present their stories. However, the congressional
study on tax reform showed Congress that it was possible
to eliminate thousands of tax rules and get to a single page
form, as well as a flat tax. This is a good place to begin.
We believe that the balance sheet, without thousands of
loopholes to favor better reporting, will make things easier to understand. Producing more accurate and verifiable
information will be a greater chore. Companies must
begin the work of creating cultures based on performance
reality where facts and accuracy rule. This will take time,
but it can be done and is being done in many companies.
Again, the IRS now processes over forty million e-filings
that are 99 percent error free. Paper filings have an error
rate of about 20 to 30 percent. Remember, though, it is
only error free if the initial numbers are right.
Nevertheless, error free is not an impossibility. Full disclosure is not rocket science. Congress and the federal
agencies wrote the books and created the forms to force
federal employees to locate their potential conflicts of
interest. They must certify and recertify where they have
financial or related interest and where conflicts may arise.
Corporate executives, analysts, brokers, investment
bankers, and many others need to do the same, but with
consequences significant enough to make a lasting
impression. Without the enforceable full disclosure rules
and the right consequences, we must assume that the
nondisclosure gang may have a problem. Likewise, real-
time reporting, executive responsibility, and the rest are
areas of solutions. Real-time reporting is a technology-
based capability that will be possible in this decade. It
should be applied to the work of performance reporting.

In their zeal for real-time reporting, some companies have made claims that they can close their books within a two-week period. Most CFOs would love to be able to close within a two-week period. The new technologies may be able to support real-time closing every twelve hours or ten days. A lot of what we want to accomplish faster depends on simplifying the rules and the processes. It makes no sense to embed our currently complex rules in an advanced technology. If we do, we will be in worse shape. This ability will someday be available to corporations to close books and report with reliable accuracy. Perhaps it should also be available to the SEC so they can keep up with the companies and the auditors. We do not have the perfectly acceptable solution for each of these areas. This is not the intention of this book. Our intention is to provoke the dialogue and get the ball rolling.

The problems we point out in capital markets, the SEC, and auditors have evolved over a complex history of nearly one hundred years. The solutions, we trust, will not take a century to develop. But the solutions cannot be reduced to a few pages of narrative. We are providing the framework for analysis, discussion, and discovery for investors to make sure they are heard as Congress and others formulate the solutions.

CHAPTER SIX

Dysfunctional Governance

For many of these companies, their boards are their number one
underperforming asset.

— Patrick McGurn, Vice President, Institutional
Shareholder Services

HOT SEATS IN THE BOARDROOM

Investors depend on the board of directors to set the strategic direction of the corporation and deliver shareholder
value. In the recent past, however, investors lost sight of
the boardroom as the center of gravity for corporate value
and performance. Most of us got caught up with investment advice from brokers and TV pundits. Now in the
post-Enron period, the boardroom is back in the spotlight.

Serving on a corporate board of directors these days
is a risky proposition. Who in their right mind would want
to do so? After the first few hundred class-action legal

cases were filed in the Enron case, many of them against the board of directors, CEOs and boards across the nation took a look at each other and what they had been doing for shareholders. Board members have become focused on their potential liabilities. We can only hope they will also focus on shareholder value.

The National Association of Corporate Directors (NACD) and other board associations have reported that boards remain confident about what they have been doing. This is not new. Directors always think they are on top of things. They had better think again. Investors are not interested in hearing from boards that they have been doing a great job when the world is awash in contradictory facts. The reality is that boards are out of touch with their companies in far too many instances, and they need to pay closer attention to investor concerns. If boards are doing such a great job, why do we see such a boom in shareholder class actions, and why don't we see a lot more reports about how great the boards are performing?

Directors have two major responsibilities. First, they are the trustees of the shareholders and have a legal fiduciary responsibility to protect shareholder interest through a governance process that directs the corporation along its strategic pathway. Second, the board has the duty and responsibility for the hiring and firing of the CEO. If boards cannot get these two things right, they cannot serve responsibly. The board of directors is the first line of governance and oversight of management activities in public corporations.

Within the corporation there are other layers and mechanisms of governance specifically designed, in most cases, to ensure that business is on the right track. Governance responsibilities spill over into the audit firms that work for the audit committees of boards. Governance responsibilities for public capital markets also reside, although this is not often recognized, with the Congress of the United States. It may not occur to directors that there is a legal chain between their responsibilities and legislative acts on Capitol Hill. But congressional authority is present, through laws and rules administered through federal agencies like the SEC. Congressional legislation is the top of the governance pyramid and the ultimate source of protection for shareholders. We would like to see this linkage made stronger through a congressional committee or subcommittee that pays attention to shareholder issues and boardroom responsibility. Directors of financial institutions are under extremely close scrutiny by Congress, and so it should be in capital markets where corporate directors have fiduciary responsibility.

Governance is not working well. The woes of the Enron board are just one example of the problems directors experience today. Boards, as a Spencer Stuart (a leading executive recruiting firm) report says, are an underperforming asset. Very few people can tell you exactly how the board adds value to the corporation. In some cases board members are brought to the boardroom for their connections and influence in the market. This is seen as a shortcut to market access and makes up for what sales teams cannot do. In other cases, directors are brought in for specific skills and experience to help the board plan and develop business strategies or other programs of management. In privately held companies, the range of types of directors is very broad, ranging from a group of insider buddies who focus on squeezing money out of the company for themselves to private companies who have stronger and better boards than the best of the publicly traded corporations.

The great unevenness in the world of corporate governance reflects the differences in legal requirements between different kinds of companies in different settings. The value directors bring to the boardroom runs from negative and significant risk to very high value at the strategic level. You just never know what you might find in the boardroom. Enron probably had a mixture of both high-value and negative-value directors a few years ago. But, as a TV reporter noted, after reading the minutes of the Enron board, "There is no doubt that they knew what was going on." Over time a board begins to bond and to create its norms of team play. Boards who do not take critical reviews of what they are doing can drift off the edge of their fiduciary responsibility into shareholder lawsuits.

The standards for board performance are all over the map. Some are evaluated, most are not. Some have strong processes and follow the good governance guidelines or exceed them. Most do not. No certifications are required for board members other than the blessing of the sitting board to join their team. Some boards treat potential or actual conflicts of interest under strict rules; others pay little attention. Boards with the latter should not make investors feel excited about how well their trustees are looking out for shareholder value. Boards should be one of the prime intellectual capital assets of the corporation, and their insight into the best practices in business should set a high standard for conduct at the executive level. There are several outstanding boards where this is the case. However, the average investor knows little about the boards of the companies in which they invest. Boards do not communicate effectively with investors, and investors view the boardroom as a mysterious place where strange things take place. It is the least effective communications arm of the corporation.

Boards have a serious set of challenges ahead. It is becoming more difficult to attract the right talent to the boardroom in the post-Enron period. Yet boards need to freshen their perspectives more often these days with bright new talent with brilliant backgrounds. Entrenched, lockstepping, narrow-minded directors cannot produce value for investors. Investors now want to know how boards are going to configure themselves for the perpetual creation of value in the markets.

Building strong performing boards may become the most important work of corporations, and the most challenging. It was not very long ago that business executives called the executive recruiting firms to let them know of their high interest in serving on a board. Becoming a director was viewed as a major career mark for a rising business star. For senior business executives and retired CEOs, board seats were the transition to retirement. In some cases, directors became "over boarded," and there are plenty of examples of well-known businesspeople serving on twelve to fifteen boards. They made a lot of money and gave each board a minimal amount of time and attention.

The board practices of the large search firms (Heidrick & Struggles, Korn Ferry, Spencer Stuart) were very active and vocal about director recruiting over the last five years—each of them made claims about their placements and their deep experience in the boardroom. These same recruiting companies, whose own boards were never known for outstanding value creation, were thought to be real experts on governance and the work of directors and are responsible for placing a large number of directors at the largest corporations in the world. Search firms probably know a lot about CEOs and board members and the rituals of bringing a new member into the tribe. However, director recruiters will require a new process to support the identification of director talent for the future. The point search firms have missed is that acquiring good director talent is more than finding an acceptable person that other directors will like. Director recruiting is a process that begins with a deeper under-standing of the corporation and its governance model.

The pathology of the Enron board provides a good case study for the difficulty of getting the right talent with the right focus. At first glance, the credentials of the Enron board looked great. But while it had the image of credibility, it didn't have the substance. The Enron board met frequently and had all the right committees and the trappings of independence. They had strong guidelines for executive and director evaluation. On the surface, this board would have been judged to be well within the good governance guidelines. This is scary since below the sur-face shareholder value was being destroyed, and there were no boardroom interventions to stop it.

The Enron board members did not bring the critical eye and the probing questions to their work. In a real sense, the concepts of good governance can be a trap. A simplistic checklist of good governance traits can give the appearance of compliance. But there is no way for investors to get below the surface and determine the real-ity of boardroom intent or compliance. Beyond good governance, what still needs to be developed is a way to certify that board members have the capability to serve as well as a way to actually assess performance.

THE VALUE OF THE DIRECTORS' TALENT POOL

How can directors become a high-performing asset for the corporation? If they did their jobs as investors expect, they would provide the fundamental value of trust and confidence in the corporation. Yet, as we have pointed out, business models are changing faster, and directors face a more confounding business environment. Part of a board's ability to produce value for the corporation resides in the collective intellectual power, general and specific skills, and experiences. Board members are on slightly different ground these days. Technology, global business situations, and a faster changing market place different demands on directors. Still, we continue to think that if someone is a director, he or she is suddenly wise and profound in knowledge and insight. Directors are like the rest of us. One day they were running a business or a business unit, and the next day they are directors. Boards are people, mostly with expensive suits and a very big, often unrecognized, set of ethical and legal responsibilities. They are supposed to be able to perform with high effectiveness as a group and as individuals. Some of them bear the extra legal burden of sitting as independent directors. They must be able to stand against the tide when the tide is moving in the wrong direction. They must have the courage to break apart from the "groupthink" and group norms to challenge the thoughts of the day. The boardroom is a serious and risky place, and directors need more formal preparation for their work.

Some business schools (Wharton, Stanford, Duke) offer one- or two-day seminars about trends and legal issues of concern to directors. Most directors feel they do not need to waste their time since they are confident that they have all the knowledge required. About 2 percent of them do. The rest could use an awakening and exposure to a few new ideas.

The Conference Board and the NACD have been on the fence about the need for director certification. They seem to believe that existing processes for preparing trustees is good enough. But preparation is left up to directors. If they educate themselves and appear to have the right experiences, they can serve on a board. Each director is the product of his or her own career path and the perceptions of those who think directors are qualified. This is not good enough. Directors need more formal preparation.

Investors are going to demand that directors know what they are doing by understanding the difference between good governance and bad. We need new, if not perfect, ideas around the preparation of directors:

- The creation of a National Institute for Governance sponsored by, not controlled by, large investment banks, corporations, the SEC, and interested foundations. This should be the schoolhouse for new directors, and it should be a place to elevate the role of directors   and restore investor confidence in trustees.
- An expansion of the directors' colleges already in place at universities and support from corporations

by sending rising young business leaders to these places of learning.
- Director development programs for sitting boards to help them become more effective boards.

These ideas are unrealistic today because corporations have not reached a state of readiness to make changes. In time we believe that these notions will emerge as issues to explore with much greater rigor, and they will initiate the search for real avenues of change and improvements. Thus far, most of the ideas for reform have centered on rules and regulations rather than the intellectual focal point for governance, the board of directors. Until we figure out ways to elevate the thinking, learning, and strategic importance of directors, rules will not make much difference.

The SEC should have a role to play in this area of director education and certification. After all, directors are the top of the "trust chain" and the main legal link between corporations and shareholders. If directors can be assisted in the work of trusteeship, we will have a better chance of avoiding Enrons.

Corporations must be willing to invest in the education of the next generation of directors by sponsoring independent development to prepare them for their responsibilities. Independent thinking is the missing value in most boardrooms and must be restored. The universities would need to beef up their programs and figure out how to make them sustainable. Boards can decide that they need ongoing programs of development: It's up to them. Investors will be watching to see if anybody does anything to improve the readiness of boards to serve the shareholders.

PROCESS IN THE BOARDROOM

Boards are out of touch with the way business operates
and the way effective governance applies in global markets. The pace of business and the glut of facts and figures about performance are beyond the managerial
capabilities of traditional boards. Meetings four to eight
times a year are an inadequate means to break the code on
how the company is performing, especially as the size and
complexity of global business continues to increase. As
board members prepare for their half-day or one-day sessions, they receive a box of binders filled with snapshots
of data about what is going on in the company and what
the CEO is doing. If the chair or CEO is a dominating
leader, the board will follow his or her agenda and allow
for a narrow process of governance.

The narrow process develops when the board members sit back and accept the CEO agenda without adding
their own areas for discussion. This sounds trivial, but in
the pressure of time many directors are perfectly willing to
show up and accept the six points the CEO has selected
without pushing for two others of great importance. Hard
issues get deferred for later sessions or offline discussions.
This is where processes begin to break down. Boards no
longer have the luxury to do complex work in a few hours
and a quick read or an assumption that they understand
what is really going on. The boardroom must become a
place of precise understanding and verification of critical
details. It is much easier the old way, when meetings took
place at the country club in a casual atmosphere of good
times. If directors actually insert themselves into the
process, it complicates the day. Directors are at the mercy

of who fills the binders and who decides what is included and excluded in the books of information. They rarely have the time to weave through hundreds of pages or to verify what they are seeing and hearing. They achieve their independence when they can look for information on their own and make sure big issues make it to the agenda. The way boards work today, in the majority of cases, is barely adequate for the routine approvals and resolutions they face each quarter. It is not adequate for the level of governance oversight required in the modern corporation.

We know there are some great examples of very strong boards among the very large corporations. General Electric, Campbell Soup, Home Depot, IBM, and many others trade positions in the annual rankings of the best boards. They have set the pace in the area of good governance. Several large corporations, such as AMD, ADM, Disney, Cendant, and others ranked at the bottom of the list, refuse to let go of board structures, processes, and habits of the past, which have proven to be bad for shareholders. Bad boards are those who do not accept shareholder recommendations, pass out high compensations without regard to executive performance, do not meet the guidelines for independence, and allow management to run away with the company.

Institutional investors with trillions of dollars invested in global markets have been surveyed many times about their preference for good governance. Eighty percent of the large investors report that they prefer to invest in corporations with track records in good governance to those that do not practice good governance. All other things being equal, the company with the added benefits of good governance will gain the support of the large investors even if its financial performance is slightly below the others. The strategic values of good governance are well known, one being that investors have a better chance of avoiding disasters in the form of business fraud and managerial incompetence. The clout of institutional investors is beginning to work. Their rating associations are investigating boards and assigning them a grade on director performance. This is one of the best trends we have seen. But corporations still have a long way to go to meet the rising standards they will face. There is no more important focus for corporations than getting things right in the boardroom.

As with most sound managerial work, good governance practices focus on highly qualified people, sound work processes, and the development of business cultures based on hard work and integrity. A recent survey by the McKinsey & Company consulting firm defined a company as having good governance practices if it has a majority of outside directors with no management ties on its board, undertakes formal evaluation of directors, and is responsive to requests from investors for information on governance issues. Directors should also have significant holdings in the company, and a large part of their compensation should come in the form of stock options. These are the first few steps toward good governance. The directors must then invest a lot of brainpower and energy to establish the work processes, the information access and analysis procedures, and the progressive knowledge foundations to lead the corporation. High-performing boards balance their efforts between helping with the management of the company and leading the company toward change. These directors evaluate themselves and their governance structures to understand how well they are doing and what they need to do better.

The board of Campbell's has been recognized for its good governance. Their directors' evaluation process has been noted as a very important tool for improving director performance and finding out what it takes to properly support a director at work. Among the boards that evaluate themselves and their work processes, directors have found that they could improve the quality of information and analysis to understand business operations. Without these careful work process reviews, boards can become easily trapped by poor processes and weak information. Directors must sharpen their efforts to probe deeper and seek more complete understanding of business operations. They must work hard to ensure independence on the board and in the actions of the key committees. They are not perfect, but they are as good as it gets in bringing home the bacon for shareholders and doing things right. When the stacks of reform bills are lined up at the end of the Enron hearings and all the political hay has been made, it will be interesting to see how much the reforms say anything about improving governance processes. Congress can make all the new rules it wants, but until governance becomes a high value process with higher standards, the rules will mean little. If investors do not see real change at the board level, they have the biggest reason to use caution when approaching the markets. Caution, not trust, is the new investor mantra.

A THEORY OF CORPORATE VULNERABILITY

Poor governance, of course, goes in the opposite direction. Bad board cases can be found on The Corporate Library website. This website, and the board survey reports from *Fortune,* showcase the good and the bad. These reports are assessments of the best- and worst-performing boards of the top U.S. corporations. The reports carefully establish the criteria they applied in the evaluation and then rank the boards' performance. Based on the cases we reviewed and the information about how the boards performed, bad boards have a few characteristics of their own:

- They are mostly old business friends intent on cranking the company up for more money.
- They are not bothered at all by providing inappropriately high compensation for the key executives even when the company is not performing well.
- They focus on tactical data (e.g., the last report from management), rather than where things are headed.
- They do not evaluate themselves and have no interest in how well they are meeting their obligations as trustees.
- They prefer short, simple board sessions at nice places close by.
- They know few of the key managers and producers in the company.

In an April 17, 2000, *Fortune* article by Geoffrey Colvin, "America's Worst Boards," the author said, "Think of ADM's board as the Albania of Corporate America; it goes its own bizarre way, the results are terrible, and it doesn't really care what you think." Boards with inappropriate focus and incentives place investors and the corporation at risk. This is the fundamental vulnerability of the modern corporation. The boardroom is the main artery of oversight. If the main artery is clogged, the corporation will be in danger. The environment of director lethargy sets up opportunities for groups within the company to make decisions on their own, which impact the shareholders. Where boards fail to establish guidelines and ensure compliance, executives can point the company in any direction they choose. This is where corporations and their shareholders encounter vulnerabilities that appear in the form of poor management performance, wide swings in shareholder value, and pressures to stretch the truth. Bad boards provoke bad behavior to develop through the management layers. Management begins to reflect the attitudes of the board and perpetuates the culture of the board. In this sense, the corporate lie is an artifact of a system gone bad. It may also be an artifact of our overall business culture. At its core, corporate lying tells us that the values of governance and managerial oversight have been corrupted from the top to at least the middle. Notice that in these highly vulnerable corporations with weak governance structures, it is rare indeed to see a "resignation under protest." Executives who do not like what they see do not resign in ways to publicly protest bad governance and management. Most of them have already been co-opted by the system. They, like the Enron executives who resigned before its collapse, left quietly and without a sound.

At Enron, during its last days, there was at least one letter to the CEO warning about problems. It was too late, and it came from the wrong place. No board member or senior executive made a sound. The entire corporation, its system of governance and management, had been inoculated against sound judgment and even common sense. The corporation was at its high point of vulnerability. The board of directors had helped it get there. Sherron Watkins, a vice president, wrote a warning letter to the Enron CEO. This was the first written inside warning, thus far revealed, at Enron. It should have come from the board, and it should have taken place in the boardroom. The minutes of the Enron board reveal that the directors were aware and involved in the same issues that caught the attention of Sherron Watkins. She was awake; they were not.

THE CRITICAL CONNECTION

The top insiders need to tell us more about themselves and their views about integrity and business ethics. They need to tell us how the board conducts its business and how the directors are getting the company ready for the future. If corporations, with the direct help of the trustees, cannot tell us better stories in these important areas, why should anyone listen to the stories they tell about revenues, profits, sales forecasts, and the rest? It would be very interesting to see a few annual reports concentrating on a review of the leadership team and the management programs the company has in place. If directors took a more active role in communicating directly with investors, we might learn more about the "governance attitudes" in the boardroom. These direct connections between directors and investors have been frowned upon. Legal and other barriers have been put in place to keep connections from happening. Boards must consider innovative ways to relate to their shareholders. Shareholder meetings, interactive shareholder websites, special communications from the board, and other ideas should be reexamined. Shareholders want to know directors and hear from them more than they have in the past. It is no longer credible to hear from just the CEO or the chair. It is time to hear the collective report of the board as well as some of directors' individual perspectives.

Paul Gompers, Joy Ishii, and Andrew Metrick, all from major universities, developed a study, "Corporate Governance and Equity Prices," as a working paper for the National Bureau of Economic Research. They studied twenty-four ways in which a company can restrict or broaden shareholder rights. They applied instances of provisions of governance to examine the difference these provisions make in investor value. For example, under the provision of Director's Duty, which allows the directors to consider constituencies other than shareholders when considering a merger, shareholders may not benefit. These constituencies may include employees, host communities, or suppliers. This provision provides boards of directors with a legal basis for rejecting a takeover that would have been beneficial for shareholders. Other provisions, depending on how they are applied by boards, can restrict or open investor influence on the board. Provisions regarding by-laws, charters, classified boards, and many other technical rules affect investors in ways they barely understand.

The performance of companies that engaged in few or none of these restrictions was almost double that of companies with high levels of restrictions. Shareholder restrictions began to spread in the 1980s. Shareholder activism began to increase in the mid-1990s, the two factors colliding head on. The culture of restriction, according to the study, may represent some form of cultural deterioration. Where boards do not want to deal with investors or provide input on corporate conditions, there should be room for concern. If the trustees do not seek any kind of relationship with those who invest, what could be wrong? Boards who seek high levels of restrictions on investors have all kinds of reasons and excuses for their actions. The recent academic study certainly questions the real purpose of keeping investors away. If we can prove that a healthy two-way communications process brings value, why do corporations resist? For one thing, we know that boards prefer the freedom of the insular boardroom to the highly charged curiosity of investors. Investors are just a pain in the ass, according to a few directors we have met. We would like to see, in addition to better-arranged shareholder meetings, a regular process of boards communicating with investors. How boards communicate, learn, and interact will begin to define the boards of the future.

FULL-TIME BOARDS

There will be some significant changes in the ways directors manage their work in the future. They will have no choice but to play a bigger role in the ever more complex and global operations of the near future. The future showed up a few years ago when we heard members of the CMGI board talking about their "real-time board." This particular board described the complex portfolio of companies they managed through their venture's holding company. This was the world's first and leading Internet operating and development company according to the CMGI website. Every Sunday night they conducted a board meeting by phone. Every Monday the CEO of

CMGI conducted a management review with the key leaders of each business. The company had so much information, so many acquisitions in progress, and so much to do, they had no choice but to have a "plugged in" board that was nearly real-time and almost full-time. They did not like to use the primitive ways (phones) to conduct their work, but they did recognize that the work of boards is beginning to change as new business models come into existence. CMGI hit rock bottom as tech stocks fell. They found the necessity for full-time boards too late in their game.

The idea of the "real-time" or full-time board is not just another buzzword. The demands of modern boards will require more director time and new and better ways of supporting their work. Board members of the future may spend a considerable amount of time each week digesting the information that tells them about what is going on in the company. Equal in importance is the ability of the board members to keep up with what is going on through some form of knowledge management, for example, a special, secure portal. A board member would access the portal and sign into a site known as "My Board." On this secure site, the director would find all the information about his or her board. The annual schedule, all the information for board sessions, audit committees, and other responsibilities would be present on this 24/7 portal. The director could ask questions through the knowledge management utility and get coherent answers in less than one day, perhaps in minutes. The utility would collect and forward information of interest to the board members, let them know what the other directors were doing, and provide the right level of detail for their work. The information utility would also provide daily reports on SEC activity, legal issues, business fraud details, securities rules, and other information to support the directors of publicly traded companies. Boards could use technology to support online board meetings at any time around the world. They could have the knowledge, the connectivity, and the access to make better decisions. The current obstacle to even the very simple forms of technology supports for the board process is the "computational anxiety" (fear of computing and using technology) level of the majority. The generational process is still under way. We do not yet have enough board members who are articulate in the ways of information technology. They proudly proclaim that they do not need to use these computers and portals. Standing behind them is a fleet of administrative supporters who use technology for them since many cannot or choose not to use it themselves. The next generation will be more comfortable and more capable of testing the possibilities of real-time or full-time boards where they are useful.

The SEC rules on the audit committees will result in more work and attention to detail. The other committees will spend more time on compensation issues, talent development, executive recruitment, and financial verification. Boards are more often calling upon the assistance of advisory boards in many different categories to help them find the truth and the best practices in many areas. Technology advisory boards are being appended to the board of directors to help them understand and act on technology advancement for their corporations. Boards can use expert assistance on a growing number of legal issues, alliance management issues, and international business arrangements. Although the size of core boards has been reduced over the past few years, with the exception of financial services boards, the need for boards to extend their reach through the services of expert advisers is on the rise. The demands of trusteeship are taking boards in many new directions. Some have suggested that there will come a day when many directors will be full-time, professional directors. They will serve on two or three boards and this will be their full-time profession. They will help manage the growing workload of modern boards and design the value contribution of directors.

Global business models are rapidly evolving and changing and will demand governance in a particularly confusing environment where the rules of several nations apply and the concepts of what is good and right spread along a wide spectrum. The seat at the table must be a platform for action and measurable contribution. It is a seat of trust where shareholders should have better confidence than they do today that directors will keep corporations on the straight and narrow path of honesty and competence in business. So much of the story of how companies lie to investors is tied up with how well they are governed from the top. Investors will focus more of their attention at this level, and they will expect a much higher standard. Active investors will take direct aim at directors if governance is not improved or when they go wrong. We believe active investors will redefine director responsibilities and accountability in the next few years.

CHAPTER SEVEN

The Markets Have Spoken

Markets reflect, as we will say again and again, the collective consciousness of both astute professional investors and their sometimes less sophisticated counterparts, the individual investor. The prices of stocks, bonds, commodities, of all kinds of investments, as academics often point out, reflect all that can be known about the future with any degree of certainty at any particular point in time. The academics have given this notion a name: the efficient market hypothesis. It suggests that investors make their bets, if you will pardon the metaphor, based on the best information they have at that moment.

— Ron Insana, *The Message of the Markets*

MARKETS AND WARNING MESSAGES

The market, indeed, is giving us a message. The Enron case, the hundreds before Enron, and the thousands we do not know about are providing a warning to us about the governance of public capital markets worldwide. The "efficient market hypothesis" has been broken by the lack of accurate information. Millions of pensioners, whose money is in the hands of professional investors, have lost billions over the last two years. They will lose more in the future unless we fix the broken markets.

The 2001 recession was partly the unintended consequence of the inflated Internet and tech stock sectors. A large source of the inflated value of the "new economy" stocks was the hyperbole and deception that technology companies were feeding the market.

Investors around the world have tried to overcome the gamesmanship and fake signals of market manipulators through research, complex calculations, and the evaluation of management teams. However, corruption of corporate information has made the process of analysis and investment an increasingly risky business, except for the elite insiders. When the actions of corporate executives, auditors, analysts, investment bankers, brokers, and their supporters converge in processes that mislead the investing public systematically over years, we know we have arrived in new territory. The scale and penetration of corrupting market processes is global, impacting the largest of the investment banks, with losses in the billions, as well as the youngest of employees whose savings are wiped out. Placing bets as if they were at a casino is not what investors have in mind, but it is what is on their minds when it comes to the capital markets. We are in dire need of fundamental reforms since the integrity of the markets is at stake. The threats to the capital markets will be deep and wide if we do not take action to prevent the capitalists from destroying the greatest strengths of capitalism.

Investors outside of the United States have seen the American capital markets as both a paragon of power and a relatively safe haven. Now international investors with a lot of money in U.S. markets have something to think about. One is the issue of safety. Other markets, save for a few in Europe, were historic casinos where almost anything could happen because of corruption, political instability, and unpredictable corporate management. While the field hasn't been leveled because of our new "Enron awareness," we are on a different playing field. Everything depends on a strategic set of realistic reforms that restore faith in U.S. markets and begin to address governance issues in global public capital markets. Most important, we experienced our first taste of accuracy as a primary formula for the new value proposition that must be established by all companies to play in the next generation of our markets and compete for capital. If we are unable to develop real reforms to address the troubles we have known about for decades, we probably will not wake up to the fact that the entire global business model has been changing beneath our feet over the past decade. We are moving into new paradigms of business, barely perceptible at this point, that will demand new forms of governance, different legal remedies, and unusual forms of disclosure and protection. We are in a transition not yet recognized by the people who can lead change. They are focused on the Enron case, the anthill of business failure, while the elephant trails are all around us. The market has spoken. A warning has been delivered to an economic planet that may be culturally incapable of receiving or understanding warning. We have outrun our governance structures, and the free-for-all is just beginning. The investor's catch-22 lives on because the fundamental information to make decisions cannot be trusted and those who know the truth will not disclose it.

THE PARADOX OF WARNING AND REFORM

Like the warnings that preceded Pearl Harbor and the World Trade Center, the signals about the danger to the capital markets are there, just waiting for the astute, insightful observer to put the facts together. However, those with conflicts of interests are less able to see the signals. Members of Congress and expert witnesses are talking a lot about the conflicts of interest between the Andersen audit teams, their counterpart company consultants, and the clients they serve. However, Congress does not include itself in this chain of conflict. The fact that half of the House and more than half of the Senate accepted Enron political contributions, among many others, is not seen as relevant. Lobbying groups and political action committees representing the audit firms and large corporations stand at the doors of the representatives every day seeking access and influence over the laws and regulations that govern the oversight of business. The demands for full disclosure from auditors and businesses stops at that point. The much-used word of "transparency" for the corporations apparently has no place for the Congress, the PACs, the lobbyists, and the rest of the food chain of the capital markets. This highly selective approach to understanding the nature of our core problem is our first symptom of paradoxical viewpoints among those responsible for reform. The conflicts of interest, all of them, must be discovered, disclosed, and resolved as the first act of change. Without this first act, the possibility of introducing higher ethical standards into the processes of the capital markets has a low probability of success. The financial and investment processes that shape the markets are many, complex, and linked across the world. Looking at a few pieces of a few processes is the usual response to reform and one that never works.

It is not that bankers and analysts do not want some level of change. They will draw the line, as they have in the past, just ahead of where reform should really keep going. The line keeps being drawn because the interest of Wall Street players is not always aligned with the interest of investors. The "players" seek more control and more flexibility for themselves than they would allow for others. An open system of investing is not perceived to be in the best interest of Wall Street, but it really is. If, by the greatest magic of all time, we did see a solid program of reform moving to root out conflicts of interest and guarded elite positions among Wall Street investment bankers and analysts, and their executive host in the corporate world, how would we sustain the effort? The trick is balancing the goals of openness with the right kind of supporting regulations.

THE FDIC OF CAPITAL MARKETS

We need a systemic solution equivalent to an FDIC for capital markets. By this we mean not the exact equivalent of the banking FDIC, but a form of insurance to protect investors from fraud. It would be based on contributions of publicly traded corporations and federal funds. Amounts up to $100,000 per individual investor would be insured or protected in cases where business fraud or illegal insider trading caused the result in stock value. The very act of protecting investors through an insurance program would force stronger criteria for company performance and cause many more people to keep a close check on what companies are doing.

But while waiting for systemic long-term reforms, the first order of business needs to be enacting specialized reforms aimed at incentives at the top of corporations.

EXECUTIVE ESCROWS

Executive escrows for insiders in the corporations, the audit firms, and the Wall Street players involved in capital markets would prevent executives from manipulating stock for personal gain. This would, for example, have required that with every stock sale by an Enron executive of more than $10,000, the executive seller would have been required to place 50 percent of the proceeds into a federal escrow account for a period of at least two years. Audit companies would have to place 30 percent of their fee in to the same kind of account. Investment houses with large holdings would reserve 10 percent of their holdings in a particular stock under controls that prevent dumping of all their shares. After two or three years, the sellers could apply to "resolve" their escrows. This would then require a special audit of the insider traders to ensure that they had properly carried out their fiduciary responsibilities. If they were found to be at fault, they would forfeit their escrowed holdings. An audit or SEC ruling would determine if they operated properly under the law.

Every insider and director in the corporations and their audit teams would now have a very clear reason to do things right. Self-policing should be accompanied with self-bonding when you are making decisions in public capital markets. Many companies must post bonds to participate in certain kinds of work. When risks are high or public safety is an issue, companies bond themselves against potential liabilities. The same idea applies in the market. Employment agreements for executives could also include the requirement for bonding, not just directors' and officers' insurance, as a part of the employment contract.

AUDIT TAX

If auditor independence is truly the way to produce accurate audits, let's give them independence. What if corporations paid an *audit tax,* which created a pool of funds for the payment of auditors' fees? Auditors would not have contracts with corporations; they would report to the SEC and be independent of corporations who pay them for services. The SEC would select auditors for assignments to companies for a reasonable period, say, up to five years. The SEC would hold the contract directly with the audit firm, thereby breaking the tie between corporations and "their" auditors. This is real independence. The consulting side of audit firms must still be separated from audit and cannot interfere with this new form of independence. Auditors, under this concept, could also become the extensions of the SEC presence in public companies.

PERFORMANCE QUALITY PROGRAM

There needs to be a national quality program for "accuracy" in corporate information and all forms of public reporting on performance that is the equivalent of the product quality movement started by W. Edwards Deming. Every idea for reform, if not wrapped in quality, will fail to produce the level of accuracy required in corporate reporting. This is the foundation for a real performance reality program based on precise information and accurate reporting of corporate data. The information integrity of corporations has been exposed in the Enron case, and this is a critical area for big improvement.

The Baldrige awards of a decade ago can be restructured and applied to this problem. General Electric, for example, applies the highly disciplined process of six sigma that helps focus on developing and delivery of "near perfect products and services." With this quality tool one can measure how many defects exist in information or products, systematically figure out how to eliminate them, and get as close to zero defects as possible. Six sigma is a weapon in the hands of managers who want to know what is going on in business operations. It deals not only with quality on the manufacturing line, but also quality of information and certification of details. This quality approach works in some of the world's largest and most successful companies. It will work, if we apply it, for corporations, boards, the SEC, and the information they produce for investors. Self-assessment programs are a good place to start. The more courageous will invite independent quality firms to test reality with them. This is an area in which corporations should take the lead. The traditional Baldrige award program would have rated almost every firm a failure had the deep look at information integrity taken place. Corporations should take the lead in assuring investors that they are going to attend to the information integrity issues. The current standards do not hold up.

Quality programs such as six sigma, which provide codes of precision, are guided by a point of view and a belief in doing things right. The information processes that produce financial data in all categories, including sales information, should have a comprehensive set of tools for verification of data. The company should be able to produce a level of accuracy across these processes to include the data shared with supply chains, alliances, and partnerships. It really is true that executives in many companies have a hard time figuring out where they are with the financial details. For the investors this is a key managerial issue. Investors want to know that management teams can get it right, both the numbers and the ethics. Investors should inquire more frequently about both.

We all hope for the day when real-time reporting is possible, closing the books with a high level of accuracy every two weeks. In the world of business process reengineering, the financial processes have always been most resistant to change, the cover story being that the structures can't be changed due to accounting rules and the specific requirements for data capture to support reporting requirements. In other words, even in the implementation of new technology solutions, we cannot change our processes, meaning that we have the technology but can't use it. If we fail to get the processes right, it does not matter what the technology does.

If real-time, accurate business reporting works, it is possible to think about private placement and public offerings becoming wide-open information events via the Internet. Stocks and products, from initial offering to secondary offering, could be offered on the same website across global markets with no special class of insiders. This would affect the Wall Street food chain and the special interest groups who have maintained an unfair information advantage for a long time. It offers grand possibilities for capital markets and unforeseen opportunities for fraud on a new scale. Business management and administrative, legal, and regulatory capabilities are not even close to being able to support this kind of transition. However, we think it is safe to say that this is just the beginning of the kinds of changes we will see in the securities area over the next decade or two.

More new concepts about offerings, creating venture funds across global markets, and open offerings through the Internet are just beginning to surface. As the new ideas approach reality, new concepts about global accounting standards will emerge. Given the difficulties auditors have in keeping things straight today just in North America, we can imagine what it would be like across thousands of international accounting rules. Before anyone could agree whether a rule had been violated or not, another new century will have passed into history. There is some talk about setting a single international set of standards to apply to global capital markets and securities offerings, but there is not much action in place. If we follow our traditional courses of action between our ways of getting things done and the European Union's lack of agility, the rules will lag far behind business activities. This could be the next vulnerability zone for investors.

There are additional ideas for changing the equations in the capital markets. For example, let's consider the following:

- Replace the quarterly race of reporting and story-telling with a semiannual comprehensive review and report of audit. The current ninety-day crisis of reporting is what forces executives to manage the stock first and the business second. They don't have the time to do both.
- Initiate the end of the guidance calls and consensus on hitting numbers in the next ninety days; only real reportable performance counts. We need to hear from a company only when it has something real, accurate, and significant to report.
- Require the directors to report to investors on board performance and how it is adding value to the corporation.
- Include the management validation session for shareholders as part of the annual meeting to demonstrate the managerial focus and capabilities of the company.

We need some new ideas more than we need to be held hostage by the ideas that brought us to the beginning of a new century.

THE INVESTOR'S MANTRA

"Things have changed." This should be the investor's chant. When investors meet with their financial planners or brokers, they should repeat the chant and let them know the new rules for thoughtful investors. First, investors cannot afford to follow the herd as we all did in the late 1990s. In those days we simply took the advice we were given, we all read the same books, and we responded to the TV stock pickers. From now on, we want to know about the companies and the financial data, but we also want to know about the people running the companies. We want to know a lot about the CEO, the CFO, and the board. We insist on getting answers to our questions (those noted in the introduction). And we will keep on asking questions about the leadership, the performance reporting, and the direction of the company.

If financial planners and brokers are smart, they will begin to position themselves as the "investor's representative" to the capital markets. Some of them are making early moves in this direction. Merrill-Lynch started a new advertising campaign early in 2002. Comedian and actor Steve Martin is the spokesman appearing as a frazzled investor. He tells the story of the new programs for financial planning and investing where the company helps you determine what kind of investor you are and prepares you for the work of investing. What they are selling is moving your money under the management of professional investors. Your broker supervises the process under which you watch how well they do and make quarterly revisions to your portfolio. This is not a bad start, but it is not exactly what investors need. Investors want to know more about the companies in the portfolio and how the professionals are making sure that money is not in the hands of the fakers. The professional investors do not need to teach us how to be professionals, but they do need to add one more layer of comfort in the form of some real ratings on the companies in the portfolio. There is a lot of room for innovation in this area. Investors need to push for it.

When we deal with our planners and brokers, they operate with the advantage of superior information about the markets. Investors need to remind them that we are the clients, we are paying the fee, and we want to know the facts. Investors may also want to see that their investment advisers have a little skin in the game as well. For example, if they lead us to invest in a company that fails and takes our money because of fraud, they should share the pain in some form. In the past these advisers have provided the advice, sometimes even pushy advice, but held investors 100 percent responsible for whatever happens. This isn't right. Here is where Wall Street can make a move to demonstrate to us that they have confidence in the advice they give us, and we pay for, because they are doing their homework. This is the kind of commitment that can begin to reduce the casino effect in investing. When investors see Wall Street brokers and investment bankers taking action that helps protect investors, we will know that things are turning around. Until then, we must keep reminding them that things have changed and so have we.

Investors are now like the news announcer in the movie *Network* when he reaches the point where he can no longer stand his own involvement in a media that manipulates viewers and employees. Peter Finch makes his famous rant in the movie—"I'm mad as hell and I'm not going to take it any more." He then invites everyone listening to him to join in his chant. Soon he had millions of people shouting at the top of their lungs. This is the attitude of many investors and employees in 2002. We do not trust our system of investment as we once did, we trust few corporations, and we intend to find the information we need to make our investment decisions. If the information is not clear, we will not invest. Our economy and our innovative business culture hold too much promise for us to walk away. We want our markets back and we want them in a better condition than they have ever been before. But we are not going to tolerate things as they have been—not from companies, Wall Street, or the regulators. We are, indeed, madder than hell and we will not take it any more. From now on investors will be paying very close attention to what companies say and do. The corporate liars can count on it. The great companies will be glad of it. Capitalism may have, in the recent past, rewarded companies who get close to the edge without going over in order to produce earnings. In the future, investors will reward companies more for not needing to get close to the ethical and legal edge: to create outstanding performance and great shareholder value.

Postscript: March 15, 2002

Warren Buffett reminds us about the realities of our business culture.

> Though Enron (news/quote) has become the symbol for shareholder abuse, there is no shortage of egregious conduct elsewhere in corporate America,
>
> — Floyd Norris, "Stock Options Are Faulted by Buffett," *New York Times*, March 11, 2002.

As this book was going to press we noticed a few more developments around the world. On March 15, 2002, the *Wall Street Journal* reported that thirteen Korean companies had received sanctions because of various forms of fraud. Other news reports recorded deepening problems at Global Crossing. Qwest Communications and WorldCom came under SEC review for accounting issues, and the experts stated that the telecommunications industry has big problems with accounting and therefore they were just starting to take a deeper look at the entire industry. March 15 was also the day that Arthur Andersen was indicted for obstruction of justice. The news was filled with stories about the upcoming Andersen court case and speculations about Andersen's survival and the fate of the accounting profession. Nevertheless, this was an "up" day for the market, and there were many optimistic reports about the future of the economy.

These events gave us pause. We are even more convinced that what we began writing about in March 2001, way before the spotlight shone on these outrageous corporate behaviors, is at the heart of the problem of our current capital markets. Declarations without foundations and the lack of a verifiable "business DNA" that reflects the true conditions of a company are the core issues that the next progression in the management sciences must address.

The increasing awareness that financial engineering, rather than real business performance, has become the "product" of many businesses should make us pay much closer attention to corporations. Additionally, technological and transactional complexities that can so easily hide and distort the reality of a business are only in their formative stages of advancement. This confounding environment demands the constant diligence of investors, great companies, thoughtful and tough board members, outstanding leaders, and employees who can work their ways through the fog of the current corporate haze. We still have plenty of work to do to fix our capital market system.

Appendix

RESEARCH

The years 2001 and 2002 will go down as the years of business fraud reporting. The leading newspapers and business magazines were loaded with reports on securities fraud and every other form of business lie and deception. The *New York Times* business section was probably the most prolific and provided comprehensive reporting on the cases and the activities of the SEC. The *Wall Street Journal* is always a good source on business news and details, including the bad news about corporations and their leaders. The *Washington Post* provided great coverage and interesting perspectives. *Fortune* and *Business Week* provided in-depth reporting on the accounting and financial reporting problems. They also provided regular reports and annual ranking of the companies and their leadership. In addition to the print media, the Internet is the great new source for tracking corporate problems and performance. C-SPAN covered the hearings on their site, as did most of the network Internet sites. All of the print media have online iterative versions of their publications. But there are many other important sources, including the watchdog services. We have provided this selected set of sources for those who are interested in seeing for themselves the kind of information available on the Net. Naturally, the search engines, such as Google, provide a reliable gateway to sources.

SECURITIES AND EXCHANGE COMMISSION (SEC) — CORPORATE FILINGS

http://www.sec.gov/edgar/searchedgar/formpick.htm

This SEC site allows you to search by company name or stock symbol, type of filing, and/or year of filing. Annual reports (Form 10-K) and quarterly reports (Form 10-Q) contain a company's most recent financial statements. Check the footnotes in these documents for specific information on areas such as restructuring costs.

http://www.sec.gov/litigation/litreleases.shtml

This site contains litigation releases reported by the SEC. Case number lists the information: click on "edit," "find," and type in the name of the company. This site lists all releases for the current year and also lists archives through September 1995.

http://www.sec.gov/litigation/admin.shtml

This site contains administrative proceedings reported by the SEC. There are links to notices and orders concerning settlement of administrative proceedings. The information is listed by case number: click on "edit," "find," and type in the name of the company. This site lists all proceedings for the current year and also lists archives through September 1995.

http://www.sec.gov/litigation/aljdec.shtml

This site lists decisions by Administrative Law Judges (ALJ) on contested administrative proceedings. The information is listed by case number: click on "edit," "find," and type in the name of the company. This site lists all decisions from October 1995 to present.

http://www.sec.gov/litigation/opinions.shtml

This site lists all opinions issued by the Commission on appeal of initial Administrative Law Judges (ALJ) decisions or disciplinary decisions issued by self-regulatory organization (e.g., NASD, NYSE). The information is listed by case number: click on "edit," "find," and type in the name of the company. This site lists all decisions from April 1996 to present.

http://www.sec.gov/litigation/suspensions.shtml

This site lists recent SEC trading suspensions. Federal securities laws allow the SEC to suspend trading in any stock for up to ten trading days when the SEC determines that a trading suspension is required in the public interest and for the protection of investors. The information is listed by case number: click on "edit," "find," and type in the name of the company. This site lists all decisions from October 1995 to present.

WEBSITES FOR COMPANY INFORMATION

www.hoovers.com

Hoovers is a good place to start for company information on public and some private companies. This is also a good source for IPO information, both current and archived. There are certain portions of Hoovers that are available to subscribers only, but the company capsule, which is free, contains a descriptive paragraph on the company, subsidiary information, top competitors, stock quotes, key executives with biographical information, and links to the SEC site for corporate filings. It also contains links to Information Marketplace that provides analyst reports for purchase, current news stories mentioning the company, and press releases. To use, click on "search," click on "company," and then type in the company name or stock symbol.

http://www.corporateinformation.com

Corporate Information is a free site that offers research information on company, industry, country, research reports (free), company extensions (e.g., GmbH), research by state, and research news from around the world. This site not only gives extensive company information but also is searchable by geography.

http://cbs.marketwatch.com/news/default.asp?
siteid=mktw

CBS Marketwatch is a free site that includes information on stocks, mutual funds, the global market, and business/financial news. One of the features is NewsFinder, which allows you to search by company or stock symbol for Marketwatch news, news service, press releases, market advisers (fee for analyst reports), and news search. There is also an IPO feature, which allows you to search on IPO filings, after market reports, best and worst IPOs, and more.

http://money.cnn.com/

CNN Money is a free site that offers a good source of business and financial information. You may search by typing in the company name or stock symbol. One of the features of CNN Money is a rate of return calculator, which will calculate the exact percentage of return, both total and annualized, for any investment over any period of time.

http://www.usatoday.com/money/mfront.htm
USA Today Money is a free site that gives comparable information to the above sites, but also offers a link, under Investors Tools, to Bloomberg.com. After typing in the company stock symbol, click on "more information." When the company information appears, Bloomberg news and press releases on the company will appear. Access to Bloomberg through this site is free.

http://quote.yahoo.com
This is the Yahoo finance site, which gives quick quote information. Once in the quick quote company information, if you click on "More Info," you will have access to charts, news, profile, reports, research, and an insider market bulletin board.

http://fm.thecorporatelibrary.net/update/search.htm
The Corporate Library is a free site searchable by company name or stock symbol. This site gives corporate information and also information regarding the CEO, including information containing the terms of the CEO's employment contract.

http://www.oasismanagement.com/glossary
Barkley's Comprehensive Financial Glossary is a free site that offers a dictionary of financial terms. The definitions are written in plain English, clear and easy to understand.

ASSOCIATIONS

http://www.cii.org

Founded in 1985, the Council of Institutional Investors is an organization of large pension funds that addresses investment issues affecting the size or security of plan assets. Each fall, the Council of Institutional Investors releases a list of under performing corporations, known as the "Focus List."

http://www.cii.org/focus.htm
http://www.marketspan.com/states/LAWCOM/RecentCases.asp?Brand=LAWCOMLIT

This link is to Law.com, which contains a list of recent civil cases filed in U.S. District Court, by state.

ARTICLES

http://www.businessweek.com/magazine/content/01_48/b3759001.htm

Cover Story—November 26, 2001, *Business Week:* "Confused About Earnings?"

Good article that explores the differences between GAAP standards and pro forma accounting, and the different ways earnings can be reported. Contains "High Gloss Glossary" of accounting terms. (Table: "High Gloss Glossary")

http://www.businessweek.com/magazine/content/01_20/b3732001.htm

Cover Story—May 14, 2001, *Business Week:* "The Numbers Game—Companies Use Every Trick to Pump Earnings and Fool Investors. The Latest Abuse: 'Proforma' Reporting."

OTHER WEBSITES OF INTEREST

http://www.HowCompaniesLie.com
http://www.HowCompanies.com
http://www.RandomHouse.com
http://www.CrownBusiness.com

Index

employees as victims of, 92
ethics code, suspension of,
  100–101
executive responsibility at, 109,
  113
PR and advertising, 133
rise and fall of, 66–69
special purpose entities, 106
Ericsson, 40
Ethics, 16, 100–101
Executive escrows, 169–170
Executive responsibility, 109–115
Exxon-Mobil, 76

Fastow, Andrew, 31, 78
Federal Aviation Administration
  (FAA), 53
Ford, 57, 76

GAAP reporting, 38–39, 40
Gateway, 135
General Electric (GE), 76, 124,
  153, 171
General Motors (GM), 76
Gladwell, Malcolm, 46–47
Global Crossing, 13, 71, 178
Global economy, 83–85, 105–107
Gompers, Paul, 159
Governance, 144–145. See also
  Boards of directors

Hacker attacks, 84–85
Health care fraud, 58–59, 72
Heidrick & Struggles, 147–148
Hoffman-LaRoche LTD, 60
Home Depot, 153

IBM, 39, 76, 153
Identity theft, 83
Information exchanges, 118–128
Information gap problem, 75–76,
  137–139
Information warfare, 84
Insana, Ron, 120, 164
Insider trading, 34, 62
Internet fraud, 83–85
Investors
  catch-22 of, 14, 68, 166–167
  evaluation of corporations,
    15–18, 47–50

fraud insurance for, 168–169
information needs, 77–79
new assertiveness of, 174–177
verification system for, 89
warning system for, 79–82
IPOs, 43, 124–125, 127
Ishii, Joy, 159

J.P. Morgan company, 67, 91–92
Juno, 135
Justice Department, 19, 58, 71

Kelleher, James B., 65
Korn Ferry, 147–148
KPMG, 41, 90

Lawsuits against corporations,
  57–58, 61–62
Lay, Ken, 24, 26, 77–78, 93–94,
  113, 117
Lernout & Hauspie, 41
Lucent, 40
Lying by corporations. See
  Corporate dishonesty

Mackey, Sue, 99
Marketing plans, 114–115
McClenahen, John, 38
McKinsey & Company, 154
McLean, Bethany, 78
Media coverage of business, 38, 54,
  134
  conflicts of interest in, 118–124,
    126
  corporate dishonesty and, 79–81
Merrill-Lynch, 175
Metrick, Andrew, 159
Microsoft, 31
MicroStrategy, 62–63, 87, 94–95
Morgenson, Gretchen, 35, 37
Motorola, 39, 40
Murray, David, 110

National Association of Corporate
  Directors (NACD), 144, 150
NBC, 124
Network Associates, Inc., 39
Nokia, 40
Norris, Floyd, 178
Nortel, 40, 71

About the Authors

A. LARRY ELLIOTT has forty years of leadership and management experience in business technology and strategy development. After completing his B.A. at Oklahoma Baptist University in 1965, Mr. Elliott joined the United States Air Force. He completed a twenty-year military career that included combat duty in Vietnam, faculty duty at Air University, several assignments as a unit commander, and assignments as a senior intelligence officer. He left the Air Force in 1985 as a colonel and became president and chief operating officer of Management Logistics International. Mr. Elliott created his own company, Pacific Systems, in 1988. Over the past seventeen years he has been a senior business leader in several major companies. In June 2001, Mr. Elliott retired as a senior partner at Heidrick & Struggles after nearly seven years with this leading executive recruiting firm. He completed an M.A. degree at St. Mary's University and postgraduate work at Georgetown University in Washington, D.C. In

1981, Mr. Elliott received an award for his article, "The Gatsby Effect in U.S. Strategic Affairs," published by Air University Review.

DR. RICHARD J. SCHROTH is a highly respected business and technology strategy thought leader who provides powerful and strong perspectives to corporations around the world. As an international presenter on management issues and the application of emerging technologies, he is a frequently requested keynoter at major conferences and events. Dr. Schroth is no stranger to the business community, having more than thirty years of experience directing strategic technology initiatives; he is also well known for his work in business strategy and emerging technology development. He has served as a private advisor to a wide range of top CEOs and executives worldwide including Marriott Corporation and Computer Sciences Corporation. Recently featured as one of the nation's leading chief technology officers in "*Inside the Minds: Leading CTOs,*" by Aspatore Books, Schroth co-mingles insightful technology understanding with major business trends to produce actionable strategic insights that have influenced many of the Fortune 500 corporations. Dr. Schroth sets a clear course for tomorrow's corporations and dissects the future of technology and its impact on how we do business. He holds a doctorate from Indiana University, an M.S. from the University of Illinois, and a B.S. from Western Illinois University.